MONASTERY
Praise for MORNINGS

"In July 1847, Mormon pioneers famously arrived in Utah. A century later in July 1947, some Catholic pioneers followed in their footsteps: Trappist monks bent on creating a contemplative monastery, Holy Trinity Abbey, in the unlikely soil of Mormon country. In this affectionate, winning memoir, Michael O'Brien captures the expansive spirit of late twentieth-century Catholicism in America and the loving warmth of the monks who befriended him."

—**Jana Riess**, author of *Flunking Sainthood* and *The Next Mormons*

"The author of this charming volume combines his life's story with that of the famous Utah Trappist monks. A consummate storyteller, O'Brien shares his remarkable journey by weaving the tale of the Abbey of the Holy Trinity monks with his own search for a life of belonging and meaning. The final result is as entertaining as it is enlightening. An extraordinary contribution and achievement."

—**Br. Columban Weber, OCSO**, Abbey of Gethsemani

"*Monastery Mornings* is as much a memoir about a sensitive Irish American boy's journey into manhood as it is an unabashed love letter to Huntsville, Utah's beloved Trappist monastery. O'Brien's detailed history of the monastery and endearing portraits of the monks who helped raise him provide a compelling backdrop to a compassionate, brave personal narrative that both amuses and inspires."

—**Jennifer Napier-Pearce**, former executive editor, *The Salt Lake Tribune*

"Michael Patrick O'Brien writes, 'For me, one of the light's most recognizable garments is the simple black and white robe of a monk, and the light's ever soothing embrace is the sweet memory of my monastic mornings.' In that sentence, he sums up his decades-long adventure with the spirited monks of Holy Trinity Abbey, a Catholic oasis in the middle of Utah's Mormon country. He was fortunate to come of age under the tutelage of Trappist monks, and to enjoy close relationships with men who choose the search for God over the more mundane lures of the world. O'Brien began visiting Holy Trinity in 1972 at the age of 11 at his mother's urging following his parents' divorce. The abbey remained a constant in his life until its closure in 2017. This beautiful memoir portrays his monastic friends as both exceptional and ordinary, holy and altogether human. In doing so, O'Brien reminds those of us who have been hanging on by our fingertips to why we still love the Catholic Church and what it is called to be: a place of service and mercy. A place where, like Holy Trinity Abbey, the core message is love."

—**Judith Valente**, co-author of *How to Be: A Monk and a Journalist Reflect on Living and Dying, Purpose and Prayer, Forgiveness and Friendship*

"Since their 1947 arrival in Huntsville, the Trappist monks have had a profound impact on the Utah community. Their lives of prayer, simplicity, hard work, and hospitality brought their monastic traditions to the people of our state and made a great difference in so many lives. In this thoughtful memoir, Michael Patrick O'Brien makes sure the legacy of the Trappists will remain, despite the closure of their monastery in 2017. His experience living with the monks as they prayed and sang the Divine Office, worked in the fields or their small gift shop had an impact that supported him emotionally and spiritually in difficult times. This is a tribute to Utah's Trappist monks and a reminder of their positive influence on Michael O'Brien and numerous others during their presence here."

—**The Most Reverend Oscar A. Solis, DD**, Bishop of Salt Lake City

MONASTERY MORNINGS

My Unusual Boyhood
Among the Saints and Monks

MICHAEL PATRICK O'BRIEN

PARACLETE PRESS
Brewster, Massachusetts

With love to my mother, to my wife, Vicki,

to my children, and to the rest of my family

(immediate, extended, chosen, and monastic).

2021 First Printing

Monastery Mornings: My Unusual Boyhood Among the Saints and Monks

Copyright © 2021 Michael Patrick O'Brien

ISBN 978-1-64060-649-4

Library of Congress Cataloging-in-Publication Data
Names: O'Brien, Michael Patrick, 1961- author.
Title: Monastery mornings : my unusual boyhood among the saints and monks / Michael Patrick O'Brien.
Description: Brewster, Massachusetts: Paraclete Press, 2021. | Summary: "A memoir of a young boy from a broken home growing up with a colorful community of Trappist monks, where he learned to live life as a man of faith, hope, and love"-- Provided by publisher.
Identifiers: LCCN 2021012472 (print) | LCCN 2021012473 (ebook) | ISBN 9781640606494 | ISBN 9781640606500 (epub) | ISBN 9781640606517 (pdf)
Subjects: LCSH: O'Brien, Michael Patrick, 1961- | Catholics--Utah--Biography. | Trappists--Spiritual life. | Cistercians--Spiritual life. | Monastic and religious life--Utah.
Classification: LCC BX4705.O213 A3 2021 (print) | LCC BX4705.O213 (ebook) | DDC 271/.12502 [B]--dc23
LC record available at https://lccn.loc.gov/2021012472
LC ebook record available at https://lccn.loc.gov/2021012473

10 9 8 7 6 5 4 3 2

Published by Paraclete Press
Brewster, Massachusetts
www.paracletepress.com

Printed in the United States of America

CONTENTS

MONASTERY MORNINGS

Two Hugs

T HE CHILD RAN UP THE AISLE, LAUNCHED HERSELF AT THE BURLY MAN in front of her, knocking him off-balance, and hugging him joyfully. I watched quietly from just a few yards away.

At another place at some other time and with different people, such a demonstration of affection would be charming, but not unusual. This time, however, the man was a Catholic priest, the place was Sunday morning mass at St. Thomas More Church in Cottonwood Heights, Utah, and the time was the first depressing tidal wave of child-abuse revelations that rocked the United States Catholic Church in the early years of the twenty-first century. All this made the event both extraordinary and profound, at least for me.

My mind rushed back to another morning, several decades earlier, when I was a child visiting a different church. I was at the chapel of the Abbey of Our Lady of the Holy Trinity, a small and isolated Cistercian or "Trappist" monastery in rural Huntsville, Utah. The surrounding Ogden Valley (and indeed, my home state) was populated mostly by members of the Church of Jesus Christ of Latter-day Saints, formerly called the Mormons and now commonly called the Saints, many of whom were good friends with the monks. This valley of monks and saints was a beautiful place, but one with very few Catholics.

The monks celebrated Mass each morning at 6:20 a.m., a daunting time of day for a night owl like me, but a spiritual appointment my Irish-Catholic mother had strongly recommended I keep during a troubled time in our family life. My parents had just divorced, my mother was worried about the impact on me, and she had started visiting the monastery, hoping I might develop a friendship with the good monks. So, although it still was dark outside, I forced myself out of bed early on that day when Mom beckoned. I fell back asleep during the 45-minute drive to the abbey. I woke up again as our car stopped in the small parking lot near the monastery building, surrounded by the monks' farm, both nestled in the middle of rolling hills and imposing mountains.

We attended Mass together, sitting in the back of the church. As a young male, I was allowed to gather with the monks around the altar at the front of their chapel for part of the liturgical service. It was an honor, but an intimidating one. I was the only non-monk there, and I also stood out for my lack of height—two rather unappealing circumstances for a self-conscious preteen. Because I thought that monking was a rather serious business, I also did not know if the Trappists really wanted a little kid on the altar with them.

My worst fears seemed confirmed on the day in question. An old monk I barely knew by name glanced down and scowled as I stepped up to stand around the altar beside him. Time seemed frozen. I agonized about whether to slip away quietly and return to the back of the church where children like me belonged. Just a few moments later, and before I could retreat, the presiding priest announced the moment of the Mass called the sign of peace. The old monk turned and shuffled over, his scowl replaced by a broad smile. He gave me a gentle hug. Looking directly into my eyes, he said, "Peace be with you!"

As he did, the sun rose over his shoulder, and bright red, blue, gold, and green streams burst forth from the chapel's large stained glass window. The light mesmerized me. The colors seemed to dance around and embrace us. It was the dawn of my monastery mornings.

■ ■ ■

CHAPTER 1
Still Point

A TRAPPIST MONASTERY IN A QUIET, ISOLATED, AND RURAL CORNER OF one of the least populated of the United States is not the typical hangout for a preteen American boy. Yet, there I was.

Not only was I at the monastery, but one morning I was also talking to someone the monks had described as a well-known theologian, scholar, and writer. I wish I could remember his name. It was the 1970s. He was visiting there to lead a multiday retreat for the abbey's three dozen monks. I was there visiting the abbey with my family.

Perhaps just to be polite, the famous theologian struck up a conversation with me. As we chatted, we stood on the carefully tended lawn just outside the large green rounded-top Quonset hut that served as the monastery's main chapel. The conversation was mainly casual small talk. The theologian noted the abbey's beauty. Set on 1,800 acres of lush mountain farmland and hills in the rural Ogden Valley under the watchful eye of Mount Ogden, the monastery indeed was a lovely place.

I was a good conversationalist for a preteen, perhaps because of my Irish heritage, genetic blarney implanted in my DNA. I also was a voracious reader, arming me with a ready arsenal of surprisingly clever things to say that one might not ordinarily expect to hear from someone my age. A few weeks earlier, I had read a promotional pamphlet about the abbey in the monastery bookstore. A phrase it used to describe the abbey caught my attention.

I did not know exactly how to respond when the theologian commented on the magnificent setting for our casual conversation. So, I simply repeated the descriptive comment I had read in the monastery pamphlet, to remarkable effect. The conversation stopped suddenly. The theologian paused and looked at me with an odd expression on his bearded face. He seemed surprised and a little impressed.

Or maybe he just thought I was a shameless plagiarist, because he asked me, politely, if I knew that the words I had just mindlessly repeated like a parrot were from a famous poem written by a well-known poet. Of course, I had no idea about either the poem or the poet. I just liked the words and the phrase. I had assumed that T. S. Eliot was just some guy like me who had visited Holy Trinity Abbey and been fortunate enough to get his name and clever comment reprinted in the monastery's brochure.

Looking back at my conversation now, many decades later, my preteen self deserves more credit for insight—accidental as it was—than I gave him then. That young man somehow recognized, perhaps subconsciously, that he actually was standing at "the still point of the turning world."[1]

CHAPTER 2

Good Turns

In T. S. Eliot terms, during the years before we first visited the monastery, my life was much more "turning world" than it was "still point." There were some good turns and some turns for the worse.

During the good times, I considered us to be a normal, but interesting and colorful, family. The interesting and colorful part started with my mother, Kathleen Mavourneen ("Kay") Gleason O'Brien, raised by a hardworking, blue-collar family in Burlington, Vermont. Mom's mother was Catherine Helen Sullivan Gleason, a kind and loving parent, but also a proper, hardworking, and no-nonsense sort of woman. A devout Catholic, she never missed Sunday Mass.

The family lived on Peru Street in Burlington's Old North End just a few blocks from the Immaculate Conception Cathedral, the local Irish Catholic church. Early on Sunday mornings, long before anyone needed to leave the house to get to Mass on time, Catherine was impeccably cleaned and dressed, sitting in the family car, waiting, and tapping her foot impatiently. At regular intervals, she would loudly call out, "Time!" as the rest of the Gleason clan scrambled to get ready and out the door. Alas, Catherine did not get much time herself. She died in 1939 at age forty-six of coronary thrombosis. Mom grew up without her mother, ironic and sad because Catherine's mother, Kate Leonard Sullivan, died young too, in 1892 at age twenty-five shortly after giving birth to Catherine. Like mother, like daughter. Mom was only nine years old. Her world exploded when she was in the third grade.

She adored her surviving father, Henry Francis Gleason. Henry was of medium height and build with light-colored hair and blue eyes. He was a sweet, kind, loving, and gregarious man who enjoyed singing. What he lacked in formal schooling—completing only the eighth grade—he made up for in hard work as a tradesman, in Mom's words, as a "meat man." He cut and sold meat. His wife, Catherine, was the backbone of the family, and her death crushed poor Henry. Within a span of thirteen months, Henry lost not just her, but also both of his parents. Devastated, he turned to self-medication, a common Irish pain prescription. His alcoholism strained the various Gleason family relationships, especially between Henry and my mother's older sister, Mary, who was in her early twenties and just finishing school at Trinity College. Henry hit her at least once when drunk. To make matters worse, all this occurred during the Great Depression. Within a short time, he was out of work and bankrupt. A few years later, Henry Gleason disappeared altogether. Mom often told us she never knew what ultimately became of him. This mystery always haunted her.

At age ten or eleven, Mom moved to Mount St. Mary's Academy, a boarding school operated by the Sisters of Mercy order from Ireland. The red-brick, five-story school with a bell and watchtower sat on a lush, wooded lot at one of the highest points in Burlington. Henry's sister and Mom's aunt, Mary Gleason, was a nun there from 1904 until she died in 1959. Her name was Sister Mary Catherine, and she helped facilitate the enrollment of her young niece. Mom lived there for several years. Some of the sisters were harsh, difficult, and strict disciplinarians, but others treated Mom as a younger sibling, with generous and sincere affection. Mom stayed at the boarding school during holiday breaks, but one sister always made sure Mom had gifts like the other girls.

Mom's affection for the Sisters of Mercy did not stop her from engaging in mischief at the convent now and then. One escapade involved a bold attempt, with friends, to leave the school for some kind of a late-night outing via the girls' second-floor dormitory room. The conspirators tied sheets together and hung them out the window. Mom climbed down first only to find a tired, unhappy, and very stern-looking nun holding the other end of the sheet rope at the bottom. Another time, Mom and a friend mixed up all the nuns' individual prayer books. A nun's prayer book was akin to what a person's smart phone is today, holding all sorts of personal notes, pictures, letters, meditations, and prayer cards. Comic chaos erupted as the sisters, each in her full-blown, traditional, black-and-white habit, wide wimple, and veil, anxiously scrambled about the chapel trying to find their own books. Mom and her accomplice watched hidden away nearby, simultaneously thrilled by and fearful of the bedlam they had caused.

The main stabilizing force in Mom's life during these tumultuous years was her "Uncle Father Leonard"—her mother's uncle, Thomas J. ("T. J.") Leonard. Father Leonard was born in Ireland in 1871 and immigrated to America from Limerick as a young man. He attended the Grand Seminary in Montreal, Canada, and was ordained a Catholic priest in 1902. He said his first Burlington Mass at the convent of the Sisters of Mercy and worked as a priest for almost fifty years. He served for thirty-four years as pastor at the Assumption of the Blessed Virgin Mary parish in Middlebury, a small town about thirty miles south of Burlington, retiring from active ministry in 1949. After retirement, he lived in Burlington with his younger brother John Leonard, a retired lumber worker who also was my mother's godfather.

Mom adored her Uncle Father Leonard, and the feelings were mutual. He gave his great-niece the lovely but awkward, obscure, and intensely Irish middle name of "Mavourneen," which means "my darling." After her mother died, she visited him often in Middlebury and stayed in his home. Uncle Father Leonard always called her by her full name—Kathleen Mavourneen. He would use his Irish tenor voice and sing to her the 1837 love song—written by the American Frederick Crouch, but also popular in Ireland—called "Kathleen Mavourneen." I still can hear Mom telling the story. Her uncle would sing the first verse, and young Kathleen Mavourneen would smile with delight, and so he would continue singing. For a child bereft of parents at such an early age, the song helped create a much-needed sense of self-esteem and family, so Father Leonard kept singing it to her.

Because of Father Leonard's busy ministry and civic life, when Mom visited Middlebury, her care sometimes fell to others, such as Mary Leonard, Father Leonard's older sister. Also born in Limerick, Aunt Mary was the oldest of the Leonard family daughters. She migrated to America alone in 1882, the first of the Leonard family to do so, and eventually worked as a domestic housekeeper for the family of Ezra Brainerd, the president of Middlebury College. Brainerd helped Mary save her money and encouraged her to bring the rest of her family across the Atlantic too, and this finally happened in 1888 when the remaining Leonards arrived, including Mary's sister Kate Leonard (my own great-grandmother). During most of the years Father Leonard served in Middlebury, Mary Leonard—who never married—worked as the devoted cook and housekeeper for her brother and the local priests.

When Mary Leonard was busy keeping the rectory in order, the task of entertaining Mom fell to one of the other, more-junior priests also assigned to work at the parish. One was Father Frederick R. Wilson. He was ordained in 1942 and was assigned immediately to work as Father Leonard's assistant. Entertaining Mom typically meant taking her to the cinema to see Saturday cowboy movie matinees, with popcorn and candy. Mom always said that Father Wilson was a good sport about it, even though he likely had more pressing parish business to which he should have been attending. Father Wilson and Mom developed a strong bond of friendship watching Gene Autry, Roy Rogers, and Dale Evans.

During the later World War II years, Mom moved with her older sister Mary Gleason Winslow into a small apartment on Maple Street while Mary's new husband was off to war. Mom's favorite form of entertainment there was to call the elderly women across the street, sisters Mame McCarthy and Annie O'Brien, tell them a blackout was on, and then watch them scramble to close all their heavy drapes. Such shenanigans caught the attention of Annie's grandson and my father Kevin Peter ("Obie") O'Brien.

Kevin O'Brien was born in New Rochelle, New York, and moved to Vermont with his own family just a few years before he met my mom. They became high school sweethearts and got married in 1951. My father was just embarking on an Air Force career, starting as an enlisted serviceman. His father, who died just after I was born and whom my father rarely mentioned, was Donald Raymond O'Brien, a newspaper reporter and columnist. My father's mother, Florence Duffy O'Brien, was a proper, tall, and athletic woman raised near New York City. Florence's sisters married wealthy businessmen, one of whom was close friends with the great baseball player Babe Ruth. Don and Florence O'Brien, however, had their share of economic troubles. One family member used to tell how at times they were so poor that they would eat the insides of their potatoes on Monday and then eat the outsides on Tuesday. That's an exaggeration, of course, but a fine one.

Like my mother, my father descended from a long line of Irish Catholics who had settled in Vermont and other parts of New England. Both sides of the family tree include other Gaelic Irish surnames such as Sullivan, Leonard, McCarthy, Flaherty, Fitzgerald, and Kennedy, but also the odd name of Coolon. It is a French-Canadian name that, based on unconfirmed legend (meaning it may be just a good story instead of true), snuck into the family tree when a poor but ambitious great-grandfather wooed and married the daughter of the well-off Irish family for whom he gardened. Waves of Irish migration through Canada, first at the end of the Napoleonic wars in Europe and then during the potato famine in the mid-1800s, made Burlington the largest city in Vermont.[1] The New England writer Nathaniel Hawthorne, author of *The Scarlet Letter*, once wrote about these Celtic immigrants "lounging" around the Burlington docks, "swarming in huts and mean dwellings" and "elbow[ing] the native citizens out of work," complaints with perhaps a touch of Yankee snobbery.[2]

I have joked that Irish DNA hardwires us to eat potatoes often, in fear of another famine, but the great hunger was nothing to joke about. It was a horrific and catastrophic event, caused by a mold that destroyed the entire plant and blackened entire crops of potatoes. This happened in field after field, wiping out much of the main source of nourishment for many, and triggering an Irish diaspora that included my relatives. A million sons and daughters of Erin died of starvation, and another two million left the country, about half of them to North America. Today, there are seven times as many Irish in America as there are in Ireland.[3] The arriving Irish, according to Vermont historian Vincent Feeney, took jobs that "didn't take a lot of skill—just a strong back."[4] It was from such strong backs that my own family descended. They worked as farmers, janitors, gardeners, meat cutters, railroad workers, laborers, tailors, milliners, and store clerks.

My own parents were just twenty years old when they wed in the intimate setting of St. Patrick's Chapel adjacent to the Cathedral of the Immaculate Conception in downtown Burlington. There seemed to be a lot of love in the relationship when it started. When they were engaged in July 1951, Mom was an "office girl" at General Electric and my father was a private stationed at Lowry Air Force Base in Denver. My older cousin Michael Winslow was the wedding ring bearer and recalls seeing my parents engaged in one of the most romantic kisses and passionate embraces he ever saw. The wedding, however, almost did not happen. My father and his family accidentally overslept that day. They were late. My mother's sister Mary urgently called the O'Brien home, woke them up, and asked if they were coming. Her call set off a firestorm of panic and activity as they rushed around to get ready. Luckily, the O'Briens lived only a few blocks from the cathedral.

Mom was red-faced and furious when they arrived, and almost changed her mind about the whole event, but she went through with the service anyway. By all accounts, the September 1951 wedding was lovely, overlooking the shores of Lake Champlain. Mom's cowboy movie-watching buddy Father Wilson performed the ceremony. Military families move a lot, and Catholic families have a lot of babies quickly. My parents were no exception to either of these general rules. My oldest sister Maureen Theresa ("Moe") arrived first. A feisty brunette, she was born in the summer of 1952 and was named after my father's older sister Maureen, who had joined a Carmelite Monastery in West Virginia. Moe was a honeymoon baby, born just nine months, almost to the day, after my mother's and father's wedding day. Mom's diligent mother-in-law counted the days, just to ensure everything was proper.

My second sister Karen Jean, also a brunette, was Moe's "Irish twin." She came along just over a year later in 1953, born in Bermuda, where the Air Force had reassigned my father. The young family of four lived on the island for about two years. My red-headed brother Kevin Peter ("Pete") O'Brien Jr. joined the clan after the growing family was transferred to Shreveport, Louisiana, in 1955. Mom often said she thought she was finished having kids at that point. Surprise! I came along six years later, a towhead born in Orléans, France, in May 1961, at the U.S. Army 34th General Hospital located in La Chapelle-St. Mesmin. My father had been assigned to work with the 7th Weather Squadron at Saran Airfield during the years before Charles de Gaulle asked the American military to leave France.

Orléans sits on the banks of the Loire River southwest of Paris, and just a short drive from Cîteaux, where the Cistercian order of the Utah monks started. One of my most prized possessions is an oil landscape painting of Orléans, featuring the 250-year-old arched stone George V Bridge that straddles the Loire River, with the majestic Cathedral of Sainte Croix in the background. Mom purchased the painting from a French artist while we lived there. St. Joan of Arc worshiped in the same cathedral shown in the painting, and later saved Orléans from an English siege in 1429. The English paid her back two years later by burning her at the stake.

With children born in New England, the British Empire, the Deep South, and now France, Mom called our family "a mini-United Nations." She was convinced, during this time before routine prenatal ultrasounds, that she would never be lucky enough to have a balanced family of two girls and two boys. So, she just knew I was a girl and planned to name me Patricia Ann. Surprise again! Thankfully, she quickly adapted to calling me Michael Patrick instead. Mom once told me—the unplanned child—I was the best mistake she ever made. She was joking, of course, but the comment has lingered, imbuing me with a sense of confidence, self-esteem, and even destiny.

I do not remember living in France, but I was speaking some French (all lost to me now) when we left there in the early 1960s. From France, we moved to Hill Air Force Base near Clearfield, Utah. The base sprawls over 6,000 acres on a plateau between Clearfield, Ogden, and a town called Layton. On Hill's twenty-fifth anniversary in 1965, the four-year-old me participated in my one-and-only photo shoot. A Salt Lake City newspaper, *The Deseret News*, ran a front-page story about the anniversary and featured photos of my father and me touring various military hardware at the base. The article described me as an "energetic freckleface." The photos show me sitting at the cockpit controls of a helicopter while sucking a lollipop, making friends with a military firefighter who was sitting high up in his fire truck, and staring at the massive wheel assembly of a C-124 cargo plane. In the cover photo, my father holds me and points out a nearby F-4 Phantom fighter jet.[5]

Despite such free publicity, my child acting/modeling career never took off, so I turned to other interests. If spending part of your day reading the encyclopedia at a young age makes you nerdy and odd, well that was me. Thanks to this pastime, I was more than ready to start school at Hill Field Elementary, a public school adjoining the base, and attended there through second grade. My parents then switched us all to the closest Catholic school, which was not very close. I rode a dark blue Air Force bus for an hour twice a day to attend third grade at St. Joseph's Catholic Grade School in Ogden. My siblings were in the high school, several miles away.

It was an idyllic and innocent time. On a family trip to Yellowstone National Park, stupid tourists like us got away with tossing breadcrumbs from the barely open windows of our wood-paneled station wagon to hungry bears standing on hind legs a few feet away. At a small trinkets shop near the park, I selected my trip souvenir—a pair of small brown ceramic bears. Only later did I realize that they were salt and pepper shakers. I still have them. Back at home, we spent most of our summer mornings outside, building mud and stick gutter dams, surrounded by miniature villages serviced by fleets of matchbox cars. As dusk approached, we ran foolishly behind a truck we called "Smokey Joe," a base utility vehicle that drove around the neighborhood giving off a white but fragrant anti-mosquito smoke. After sunset, we headed to the only movie theater on the base and sought out our friend the manager, hoping he'd give us free boxes of candy.

My teenage sisters tolerated me, but with some disdain, when Mom forced them to bring me along on their outings. When they showed their sisterly displeasure with little brother, I got revenge with pleasure, using two proven methods of annoying them right back. Method one, used when forced to hold hands, involved inserting my thumb inside their hand instead of leaving it outside as normally occurred in handholding. Method two, used when forced to walk together, involved stopping every ten or twenty feet to pull up my socks. Despite their annoyance, they also taught me how to roller skate on the concrete pad that served as our back porch. I did not pick it up quickly but at least never got seriously hurt trying.

The same is not true about my outdoor adventures with my brother. We constructed a homemade roller coaster—red Radio Flyer wagons tied together with ropes—and sent it careening down a nearby hill. On this, the coaster's maiden voyage, my wagon, second behind my brother in the lead, failed to navigate a turn, cut loose, and smashed into a telephone pole. My left foot ended up wedged between the wagon and the pole, painfully but conveniently sparing the wagon from any real damage. My brother reacted to the crash by instructing me not to tell Mom about my broken foot, and then asking if I was OK.

Beneath this facade of domestic bliss, trouble was brewing, but I was oblivious. I should have felt the approaching storm when our beautiful pet longhair collie named Laddie disappeared for several days. We later found him in severe distress. For a day or two, I saw him do nothing but vomit, eat grass, turn in circles, and walk backwards. It was agonizing watching my mother's desperate but futile efforts to save and comfort the creature who had become her closest companion during a time, unbeknownst to me, when she and my father were drifting apart. We had to put Laddie down. I heard whispered, sinister speculation in the family that someone had poisoned him.

It was a dark omen, a bad turn that arrived when I was in third grade. In some sort of odd and inexplicable episode of cross-generational déjà vu, my life—just like my mother's—was spinning off the road at age nine.

■ ■ ■

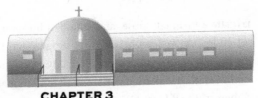

CHAPTER 3

A Turn for the Worse

THE UNTIMELY DEATH OF LADDIE FORMED THE MEDIAN PIVOT POINT of an unholy trinity of chronology for me—we were a happy family, the beloved dog died mysteriously, our family life was poisoned too.

After the dog died, I noticed that my parents argued more often than before. My father, recently back from an eighteen-month assignment in Saigon, Vietnam, was not around the house much. We were in a bad financial situation. My father's Air Force career had stalled. He was a noncommissioned officer, a tech sergeant, and was not getting regular promotions. He also was not making enough money to pay the bills. Mom was constantly on the phone fending off creditors.

She disguised our situation well, at least when dealing with me. We moved several times while my father was in Vietnam. We were not eligible for subsidized military housing while he was overseas. Some of the homes, on the fringes of the base, were less than ideal. Mom convinced me that getting dressed on winter mornings in front of the clothes dryer was a great game rather than a practical reaction to a cold, poorly heated house. She also led me to believe we sometimes had breakfast cereal for dinner because it was a fun and exciting change from our normal routine, and not because we really did not have much else to eat.

Eventually, there was a younger woman in my father's life. Of all things, she was a rodeo queen. Our family never attended the rodeo, but suddenly my father was very interested in it. My clever older sister Moe discovered the relationship and told Mom about it. In response, during a domestic confrontation my father slapped Moe. My enraged mother hurdled a table, flew at him in defense of her child, and chased him from the house. Somehow, I missed all that drama, probably because I had my nose in an encyclopedia.

I learned that my parents had separated when I overheard Mom explain the status to someone else during a phone call. In the days before everyone had cell phones, phone calls arriving on a fixed land line were a big deal, and the ringing of the phone always started a footrace and calls of, "I got it" in our family. Mom won the race on this particular day, and apparently did not see me hovering nearby. She told the caller, "My husband does not live here anymore. We are separated." I was stunned.

Perhaps because they wanted to avoid an extremely unpleasant conversation, or maybe because they thought I was too young to understand, no one told me what was happening. Yet, I had a good vocabulary, and my third-grade mind knew exactly what the word "separated" meant in this context. It meant that my cool family was splitting up. Later that same day, I saw my father in the carport. I walked over to him, convinced I had the power to fix the family problems or to make things right with a simple expression of devotion. I told him what I had heard. I said, "I love you and I always will love you." I gave him a hug. It was an act of childhood hubris, at once both spectacularly overconfident and incredibly naïve. He did not hug back.

It was one of the last times I was alone with him. Whatever short moments we spent together afterwards did not include any similar expressions of love, from either of us. Maybe it was just the natural unintended fallout from the explosion he had ignited in our nuclear family, but events that followed also suggest that maybe this was the way he wanted it. After I finished third grade, my father drove us all to Sacramento, California. Halfway there, we stopped at a motel for the night. Instead of sharing a bed with my older brother, as I usually did on family trips, I was assigned to share with Mom. "Why?" I protested. No one explained or even noted the irony that my encyclopedia-powered brain could not grasp that separating couples prefer separate beds.

We stayed with my father's younger sister, my Aunt Rita, and her husband, a successful tax businessman named Lee Baldarelli. They lived in a posh neighborhood in a large home with a lovely yard and swimming pool. Ever in a state of denial, I convinced myself that we were on some kind of family adventure or vacation. My father had another plan, however, that did not include us. He returned home to Utah. I watched him drive away . . . alone. He went back to work, back to his rodeo queen, left us all in California, and filed for a divorce.

No-fault divorce did not yet exist in Utah, so in the divorce papers my father claimed that my mother had treated him "cruelly, subjecting him to great mental pain and distress." Mom noted, with bitterness in her voice, the biting and one-sided accusation contained within his court-required explanation for the failure of their marriage. The fighting Irish spirit ran strong in her, and I suspect her first notion was to contest the allegation of "brutal" mental cruelty. Yet, she was also practical. She could not afford a lawyer and had a family to feed. So, she swallowed her pride, read the papers on her own, and signed them.

I may never know exactly why they split up. It could be they married too young, grew apart over the years or stopped loving each other for some other reason (such as, perhaps, a rodeo queen). They never really set down roots or owned a home together or were part of a community, other than the rather transient Air Force existence. Maybe it was the strain of financial stresses that blew their relationship apart. Whatever the reason, Mom was stranded in California, at the home of her sister-in-law, with four kids, no job, no money, no car, and no place of her own. The Baldarellis were kind, patient, and generous, but our presence was an awkward and uncomfortable imposition. Slicing our family in half, Mom sent Moe and Pete back to Utah to stay with my father, a painful choice thrust upon her and them by our plight.

Mom also sent me to visit my uncle for several months. Her older brother John "Jack" Gleason lived in San Marino, near Los Angeles. Uncle Jack was great, but I did not know any of his family and entered their home as a virtual stranger. His poor wife, with two adult children and a young daughter, did not know how to react to a rambunctious nine-year-old boy running around the house and getting into her things. I caused more than my share of tensions, and even burned part of her cabinet when I did not pay attention to a toaster oven I was using. I started school in San Marino, but felt homesick. Mom saved my letters, including one when I wrote that I really missed being with her, which must have been a devastating emotional gut punch from your young son. Soon after, Uncle Jack paid for my first plane ride ever, which was cool, and sent me back to Sacramento.

Mom and Karen had rented a small apartment in North Highlands, a Sacramento suburb. It was my fourth home in four months. Mom had worked part-time as cashier/bookkeeper on the Utah air base where we had lived. She found a similar job somewhere on McClellan Air Force Base. I rejoined fourth grade there, my second school of that year. Karen, an accomplished student, was trying to finish her last year of high school and should have been focused on college options, but her future, which should have been bright, was cloudy at best. Mom was riding a roller coaster of emotions—anger, disbelief, depression, rage, hurt, fear, and embarrassment—about the unraveling of her twenty-year marriage. I did not like it, but had no choice except to ride along with her.

We stayed in California for a few more months and then, in the spring of 1971, took a creepy Greyhound bus ride back to Utah. Aunt Rita later delivered the rest of our possessions. We ended up—Mom and all four of us kids—in a small, two-bedroom basement apartment in Clearfield, just outside the gates of the base. The small living space exacerbated our normal sibling tensions, which had spiked because of the family-wide trauma. We got on each other's nerves. During one argument, I threw a shoe at my older brother. He deserved it, but ducked, and so it missed him. The wall behind him neither deserved it nor ducked, leading Mom to inquire, with thinly veiled annoyance, about the new hole in the apartment when she got home from work.

The red-brick fourplex building was on a busy highway directly across the road from North Davis Junior High School. I joined my third school that year, South Clearfield Elementary School, to try to finish fourth grade. Karen and Pete went to Clearfield High School, and Karen graduated. Moe, already a high school graduate, worked various odd jobs, including at a nearby drive-in where she taught me to make Utah's famous French fries sauce when I visited. Mom's economic prospects at this stage of her life were dismal. My father only sporadically paid child support. The court file shows that in November 1971, Mom had to take him back to court and get a judgment for lots of missed back payments. Despite finally winning some meagre financial support, Mom still was a suddenly displaced homemaker in her mid-forties with only a high school education and no real work experience. She got a minimum wage job as a cashier at Andy's Chuck Wagon, a popular, all-you-can-eat buffet restaurant on Ogden's industrial west side. She got food stamps too, but she put off using them to minimize being on the dole. The government took them away because she was not using them up quickly enough.

To house and feed a family of five, Mom worked many extra hours at the restaurant, standing on her feet for as long as ten or twelve hours a day. Pete and I shared one room of the small apartment, and Moe and Karen the other. Mom slept on the couch, which was not a sofa bed, in the living room. I often woke up in the middle of the night to the sounds of her tossing and turning, crying and moaning in pain after a long shift at work.

We all tried to cope in our own ways. I poured my energy into school and into my small but thriving route selling and delivering *TV Guide* magazines to neighbors. To help support the family, Karen got a job auditing tax returns at the large Internal Revenue Service regional facility. She had been an outstanding student, despite having to attend four different high schools. Our relatives the Baldarellis had invited her to stay with them in California and also offered to pay for her to attend college there. In an extremely selfless act for an eighteen-year-old, Karen declined the generous offer and decided to come back to Utah with us and help Mom and the family.

My brother Pete hated high school. He always was better at mechanics than academics, and once built a motorcycle from scratch. When we made models as kids, he meticulously put his together. I got frustrated quickly and smashed mine. The divorce hit him the hardest. He was a self-conscious teenager who needed a father, or at least a parent, around to provide guidance. When he returned to Utah, my father may have been preoccupied with the rodeo queen and was not around much for him. Pete found some trouble with alcohol and the law. He got married in 1975, too young at age nineteen, to an eighteen-year-old girlfriend. It did not work out and they soon divorced. Three years later he married another woman, who was very nice but also eighteen and this time pregnant too. Mom refused to attend the wedding.

Moe intensified her relationship with a boyfriend and married him in 1972. Like Mom before her, she was only twenty years old and now was married to an enlisted military man. A new family friend, Paulist priest Father Frederick Draeger, performed the service. I was the altar boy. My father gave away the bride. Even I could feel the tension thick in the air. He and Mom gave Moe the best possible reception, dutifully standing by each other in her greeting line even though it was awkward. My mind, brainwashed by the 1961 movie *The Parent Trap*, hoped this event might trigger a reunion, but unlike Brian Keith and Maureen O'Hara, my estranged Irish Catholic parents both wanted to be somewhere else. After her wedding, Moe moved to California, where her husband was assigned to work in a naval hospital.

This was the turning world, the chaotic state of our lives when, one Saturday morning in the spring of 1972, Mom said to Karen and me, "Let's go for a ride."

Taking car rides must be a generational thing, for Mom enjoyed just getting in the car, and taking off into the countryside. It was an inexpensive form of recreation—gas cost only thirty cents a gallon back then—so we took many such rides. This one was different. We ended up at place I had never been. On the outskirts of the small town of Huntsville, it was called the Abbey of Our Lady of the Holy Trinity.

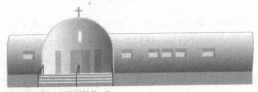

CHAPTER 4

The First Huntsville Odyssey

OUR FIRST JOURNEY TO THE MONASTERY PHYSICALLY STARTED IN Clearfield, Utah, a classic American town with a population of only about 15,000. Our hometown back then was so small that I could ride my bicycle the length and width of it and, during that ride, stop and say hello to the mayor, whose son was my friend and classmate. The mayor knew Utah's governor, Cal Rampton. One day, my friend and I called the state capitol, invoked the name of the mayor, and asked to speak with the governor. A few moments later, we were talking to him. It was the sort of phone call that probably would not happen today, a nostalgic relic from a simpler time and place when public officials more freely rubbed elbows with the people they served, even with boys too young to vote.

From that small town, we drove north, on the recently completed Interstate 15, toward Ogden City. In contrast to Clearfield, Ogden was a major metropolis. The city originally was a blue-collar railroad town, but by the time we drove through, the railroad was in decline and many of the wilder aspects of Ogden had been tamed by the steady influence of the Church of Jesus Christ of Latter-day Saints. Although it seemed like the big city to me, I also easily learned to navigate through most of Ogden simply as a back-seat driver, watching as my mother or sister drove us to the monastery. We would make this drive hundreds of times in the weeks, months, and years ahead.

As the streets passed, I would count—23rd Street, 24th Street, 25th Street, 26th Street—as we drove north to south. Driving from west to east was far more interesting, for then I encountered Washington Blvd, Adams Ave., Jefferson Ave., Madison Ave., etc. My back-seat observations later considerably boosted my American history grade when we had to name the American presidents in chronological order. I passed the test simply by closing my eyes and imagining I was driving through Ogden.

We would drive east on 24th Street and passed by eight presidential names until we reached William Henry Harrison, the ninth president. We'd turn and drive north on Harrison Boulevard, and eventually arrive at 20th Street, home to the beautiful Masonic Temple, set on a hill overlooking a public golf course. From there, it was a short ride on Valley Drive, to reach a place called Rainbow Gardens at the mouth of Ogden Canyon.

I would perk up from my back-seat perch when we approached Rainbow Gardens, wanting to stop at its Greenery restaurant and buy a delicious treat called "Mormon Muffins," hot and fresh bran muffins with honey butter oozing over them. Beyond Rainbow Gardens and the golf course, the two-lane canyon road we took to the monastery twisted and turned for about twelve miles along the route of the Ogden River. For part of the route, an old historic stone wall—probably more than one hundred years old—shielded drivers from careening into the water rushing past some ten feet below. As we drove up Ogden Canyon, we passed a couple of other memorable eating establishments. A seasonal roadside stand called The Oaks served up delicious burgers and fries in the summer months. Nearby was the regal Gray Cliff Lodge, which offered fine dining, including a wonderful Sunday brunch called the "Hunt Breakfast," so named because it was a buffet and, according to the owner, you had to hunt to find it.

We were living on a rather tight budget, and eating out was an expensive treat, not a regular event, so we usually did not stop. Instead, we continued driving up the canyon, past summer homes with river views, then on to the end of the canyon marked by an old brick water treatment plant and the Pineview Dam, built by workers from President Roosevelt's Civilian Conservation Corps. Just up a hill and past the dam was Pineview Reservoir, a popular recreational area known for camping, boating, fishing, and swimming. With Pineview Dam and then the small town of Huntsville on our left, and with the majestic Mount Ogden and the Snowbasin Ski Resort (later the site of the 2002 Winter

Olympic events) looming on our right, we continued five more miles along Highway 39 past pastures, farmhouses, and painted barns.

Eventually, on that first day, my sister spotted a road sign with a directional arrow pointing the way to something called "Monastery." With nothing better to do, we followed the arrow, made the turn, traversed a short distance past open farm fields and contented cows, and arrived at the open metal gates of Holy Trinity Abbey. We drove up and over a small hill and spotted the monastery at the end of a tree-lined road. We saw a small bookstore and went in. There were religious books and items, such as medals and rosaries, and even those funky (and somewhat odd) pictures of Jesus where his eyes follow you wherever you go in the room. The monks, called Trappists, also sold their delicious wheat bread, made from grain they grew, as well as "Mount Ogden" fresh eggs, and flavored creamed honey originating from their beehives.

The bookstore was open and quite busy. One of the store attendants was a tall, thin, and lanky monk. He wore the usual Trappist garb, which is a white robe with a black overlay hooded scapular (apron) that covered his shoulders and his torso but not his arms. His face was time-weathered and partially paralyzed on one side. He wore a military-style haircut and looked serious, but not in a frightening or unfriendly way. We would learn that his name was Brother Felix McHale.

I think Mom was looking for a particular book that day, so she turned to Brother Felix and started to ask, "Do you know what I am looking for . . .?" Before she finished her thought, he politely interrupted and said, "Yes, I do know, you are looking for the same thing as the rest of us— peace." His words were not profound, poetic, or prophetic, and the only thing they managed to do was to change our lives.

CHAPTER 5

Near to Heaven

M Y MOTHER STARTED TAKING US TO THE MONASTERY REGULARLY, sometimes several times a week. During one early visit, Mom and Karen walked into the monks' church, but I lingered behind, curious to explore something I had noticed earlier. I slipped through an unlocked wooden fence gate and walked tentatively into a small grassy field adjoining the church. Initially, I hesitated just inside the gate, but soon several small white crosses drew me further into the middle of what was the well-kept monastery cemetery. Within moments, I was standing on the graves of ten monks and reading the simple crosses marking their burial sites.

The inscriptions did not include much information, only a name and some dates, but I was intrigued. I recognized some names as Irish, including "Michael Francis Carney." Others were more exotic. I liked "Ivo Kilawee." I laughed as I tried to quickly say three times: "Tescelin Szwagdys." I saw "Antonius Maria Josephus Lans" and wondered if his Latinized names meant he was someone important. Eventually, the monastery bells started to ring, and so I left the graveyard and joined my family in the chapel, wondering, *who were these men?*

My inquiring mind eventually overpowered my concerns that I would get into trouble for sneaking into the cemetery, so I asked some of the live monks to tell me about the dead monks I had encountered. It was the beginning of a lifelong quest to know more about these unusual men into whose strange world I had stumbled. Over time, after asking questions, listening for clues, poking around the guesthouse library, and doing additional research, I learned their story.

It began on July 7, 1947. On that hot summer day, three dozen men, all members of the Order of Cistercians of the Strict Observance (OCSO), boarded a train and departed from their home at the Abbey of Gethsemani near Bardstown, Kentucky, forty-four miles south of Louisville in the rolling hill country of central Kentucky.

Their leader bore the lengthy and impressive name I saw on my first cemetery visit: Father Antonius Maria Josephus Lans, a solemn-looking priest originally from Holland but very well traveled. He had worked as a landscaper in Southern California before becoming a monk. The Gethsemani abbot, Father Frederic Dunne, joined the group of contemplative pioneers on the trip. Father Dunne's grandparents were Irish, and he was the first American to become a Cistercian abbot.[1] Accompanying the two abbots were many other monks, including some of my other graveyard acquaintances: a World War I veteran and theology professor from Brooklyn named Father Ivo Kilawee; a simple monk born in Ireland called Brother Matthew (aka Michael Francis Carney), and another Brooklyn native Brother Tescelin Szwagdys, named after a Burgundian knight also called Tescelin, the father of one of the greatest of the Cistercian monks, St. Bernard of Clairvaux.

The train and monks were headed to Huntsville, Utah, an agrarian town nestled in the Ogden Valley 1,500 miles from Kentucky. The towering, 9,500-foot Mount Ogden shelters the valley, which is nurtured by a steady flow of several forks of the Ogden River. The brothers planned to build a new monastery on ranchland they had acquired. They wanted to dedicate it to the Blessed Virgin Mary and to christen it *Abbey of Our Lady of the Holy Trinity*. Why? In the 1940s, Gethsemani Abbey was overflowing with monks, and had to reduce the pressure by exporting some of them. A fellow Trappist left behind in Kentucky—named Thomas Merton—noted "phenomenal" growth in Kentucky, with servicemen (back from World War II) "lining up four and five at a time" to trade in khaki for monk robes, observing, "There has hardly been anywhere for them to sleep."[2]

Why Utah? Abbot Dunne preferred to create new monasteries in places where the population was predominantly non-Catholic. One of his assistants, Father Gerald McGinley, wrote and told his sister—a Benedictine nun working near Huntsville at St. Benedict's Hospital in Ogden—about the monks' expansion plans. It was Sister Myron McGinley who wrote back, suggesting locating the monastery in Utah, where two-thirds of the residents belonged to the Church of Jesus Christ of Latter-day Saints, then often known as the Mormons.[3]

Intrigued, Dunne made several trips to Utah to scout out property. Foregoing his traditional robes, he camouflaged himself as a layperson, once even wearing a hunting outfit, to conceal his identity and avoid the sectarian suspicion that might arise at the sight of a monk scouting out property or seeking to buy so much land in Utah. Dunne was a hardworking abbot, involved in setting up two or three new monasteries at the same time. His numerous train trips, including to the high altitudes of Utah, taxed his heart condition, and after one of them, he suffered a hemorrhage. When someone suggested he let another monk replace him on future journeys, Dunne laughingly responded, "If anyone has to bleed for that foundation, I'm the man." He did take at least one brief break from his hard work when he remembered, during a trip out west, to collect some Utah stones and bring them back for the niece of a friend, a Kentucky businessman. The young girl had asked for a part of the Rocky Mountains.[4]

Over the course of several visits in 1946 and 1947, Father Dunne came to like the setting of the William C. Parke Ranch near Huntsville. Parke had been in the feed and cattle business. Before he owned the ranch, the same land was a co-op farm owned by the local Huntsville ward (the Latter-day Saint version of a parish). Dunne collaborated with Utah's Catholic Bishop Duane G. Hunt and with an Ogden parish priest to purchase the ranch. The owners jacked up the price, allegedly to keep the monks out, but Captain James William Kinnarney, a shareholder in—and head of police/security for—Kentucky's Churchill Downs, contributed and raised the necessary funds. The monks paid $100,000 for 1,600 acres of land, about sixty dollars per acre.[5]

In stark contrast to other places in Utah bearing names such as Purgatory Flats, Devil's Canyon, Hell's Backbone Ridge, and Devil's Slide (a massive limestone chute in Weber Canyon about a half hour's drive from the monastery), Ogden Valley was, in many ways, the perfect place to start a monastery. Just northeast rises a 9,000-foot peak called Monte Cristo—the mountain of Christ—although no one seems to know why

it has that name.[6] Drive a few miles outside Huntsville and you find
yourself in an unincorporated community called Eden. Moreover, Utah
and its dominant church frequently are associated with or even called
Zion, which in the Bible refers to the hill on which Jerusalem sat.

The monks traveled from Kentucky in two designated Pullman
train cars. One was full of monks. The other overflowed with supplies
(altars, stools, candlesticks, bookstands, vestments, books, chalices, altar
linens, cruets, and many other things) for the new abbey. The cars also
were stocked with food for the long voyage, including fruits and rolls.
Well-wishers added to the food supply during the journey, including
nontraditional monk food such as doughnuts. The monk caravan first
stopped in Louisville, and then moved on to St. Louis. In the Gateway
City, a crowd gathered at the rail station as the brothers said Mass in their
car during a six-hour stopover:

> The car had been there for several hours, and the monks were
> inside with the blinds down, and many curious people were on the
> outside in the hot sun, and one porter and three yard detectives
> were keeping the people on the outside from getting at the monks
> on the inside. Either that, or they were keeping the monks in the
> car from escaping. No one could be quite sure which.[7]

The train continued through Missouri, Kansas, Colorado, and
eventually arrived in Salt Lake City. As they rode the rails westward, the
monks tried to maintain some semblance of their established monastic
routine such as worship, prayers, chants, solitude, and related practices.[8]

They also took advantage of the sightseeing opportunities typically
unavailable to a Trappist monk. One monk observed:

> Trappists are, among other things, farmers. And they took a
> considerable interest in the corn that was growing in Missouri
> and the wheat that was being harvested in Kansas. But they are,
> above all, contemplatives: and the Rocky Mountains are nothing
> to be despised! They have something very eloquent to say about
> the God Whose power they reflect: and if the Trappists did not
> have an ear to catch that message—who would be there to hear it?[9]

Many of the brothers took to the train windows to take in the mountainous and rugged Western landscape. Awestruck, one exclaimed, "How shallow the mind of that person who said that when God came to this part of the world, he just left it all piled up. No. We are among those inaccessible heights where even angels fear to tread. This country was made to order for the glory of God."[10] Even the monastic group's stern-looking leader, Father Lans, stayed up for all of one night "looking out the window, and enjoying the beautiful moonlight reflected in the rivers and streams. He had no opportunity for such sights for many years, so it was quite a treat for him to behold the soft splendor of our Lady's mantle, the moon."[11]

After a long journey, the Trappists arrived safely in Ogden on July 10, 1947. A delegation made up of the local Catholic parish priest, Monsignor Patrick F. Kennedy of St. Joseph's Church, and other Catholic dignitaries met their train at the station. The *Ogden Standard-Examiner* newspaper welcomed them with a photo and a large headline: "Trappists Greeted Upon Arrival From Kentucky."[12] If the sight of three dozen bald, robed monks disembarking from a train in downtown Ogden was not enough to shock and worry the predominantly non-Catholic population, their baggage probably did the trick. Although teetotalers themselves, the monks had used old liquor crates and boxes to pack their stuff. "If the Mormons were paying attention as the monks detrained in Ogden, they must have been scandalized to see so many boxes labeled 'Schenley's' and 'Green River.'"[13]

Monsignor Kennedy transported the two Trappist leaders in his car, and a chartered bus carried the rest of the group to Huntsville. The caravan stopped for a moment at nearby St. Joseph's Church, and then drove the same route my family later did to get to the monastery.[14] When the pioneer leader Brigham Young first arrived in the Salt Lake Valley a hundred years earlier in 1847, he exclaimed, "This is the right place!" Similarly, when the monks arrived at the site of their future monastery some sixty miles north of where Brigham Young arrived, Abbot Dunne softly declared, "I think this place is near to Heaven, and it should be our endeavor to make it more so."[15]

The newly arrived monks were minor celebrities, sometimes uncomfortably so, among the small Utah Catholic community. On one visit to Huntsville, two women rushed up to Abbot Dunne, "and before he knew what they wanted they took him one by each arm and said, 'Look up.'" Someone took their picture. The abbot, wiping his brow, moaned, "If that ever gets published . . .'"[16] During this same visit, according to one monk's journal, "The people wanted to see some monks, so Bro. Matthew [the one and only Michael Francis Carney from my first cemetery visit] came over and told five or six of us to promenade in front of the monastery. Monks or monkeys, monastery or zoo, some of us may have thought."[17] Later in 1949, there also would be visits by Utah Governor J. Bracken Lee, Ogden Mayor Harman W. Peery, and Salt Lake City Mayor Earl J. Glade, and their families.[18]

Despite the initial fanfare, there was work to do. The monks quickly moved into three wooden surplus war barracks, previously used to house German and Italian war prisoners. The one-story buildings, moved to the site in late June 1947, each measured one hundred feet by twenty feet. The monks also began to construct a temporary monastery from corrugated metal Quonset hut materials. They installed a makeshift heating system for their wooden barracks and obtained water from a spring on their land some 7,000 feet away.[19] It was hot and grueling labor. Many of them regularly got bloody noses trying to acclimate to the high altitude. As one of the monks reported, "People speak of Trappists digging a shovel of dirt from their grave every day, well, we have done enough ditch digging to bury two communities of our size and each corpse would have a good deal of elbow room."[20]

In October 1948, the monks finally completed their temporary monastic Quonset hut building, which is the building I visited a quarter century later.[21] Unfortunately, Abbot Dunne never saw the completed project. He died unexpectedly in August 1948 while riding a train to visit another one of the many new monasteries he had established. Dunne would have been happy to know that Holy Trinity Abbey was designed and constructed in the traditional Trappist mode. The abbey, like most Trappist monasteries, "is built in a quadrangle, with each office and cloister exactly located as in all others, so that a member of one community would know definitely in any other monastery where to find everyplace where required activities would occur."[22]

The abbey church also followed Trappist norms by facing east and west. It was simple, plain, and functional, with a rounded semicircle ceiling (the inside part of the curved Quonset structure) that rose about thirty feet high. Rust-colored wooden choir stalls faced each other with two rows of seats. When we started to visit there, there were two sets of these choir stalls, but one was eventually removed. The back of the church where visitors sat was separated from the rest of the sanctuary by locked tall wooden grated gates (also eventually removed) that were about eight feet high. The front of the church included a raised altar and a spectacular stained glass window, which came to be my own favorite feature of the sacred space.

Years later, I learned the Trappists initially planned to replace the Quonset huts with a more permanent and much more splendid structure, consisting of stone quarried from a canyon on their property. They released beautiful architectural drawings of the project in 1952. The huge stone structure was designed in a twelfth-century, French Gothic style, with 90,000 square feet of space and topped off by a 232-foot bell tower. (For perspective, consider that the actual bell tower probably was about fifty feet tall.) Projections indicated that at a cost of some $30 million, the new monastery would take twenty to thirty years to complete.[23]

The *Ogden Standard-Examiner* described the proposed new monastery as a "Giant Edifice."[24] Plans called for it to sit on a nearby "hilltop that commands a vast view of the valley and the mountains."[25] However, the grand edifice was never built. In 1964, monastery leaders deferred building plans, ostensibly due to liturgical and other changes coming from the Second Vatican Council that could impact church design.[26] Funding problems also surely played a role in the decision to stick with the original "temporary" Quonset huts.

These Trappists—soon to be my friends—were part of a religious order established in France 1,000 years earlier, in a manner not unlike the founding of their Huntsville site. According to Holy Trinity Abbey's website, "in eastern France in 1098 AD, Robert, abbot of the monastery of Molesme, north of Lyon, took with him twenty monks and founded a monastery at Citeaux, which became the center of the Cistercian Order, to which we belong."[27] The word "Cistercian" derives from *Cistercium*, which is Latin for Cîteaux.[28]

Perhaps the most famous Cistercian hero is St. Bernard of Clairvaux, a twelfth-century French abbot, writer, scholar, and preacher canonized in

1174 as the first Cistercian saint. St. Bernard appears as Dante Alighieri's last guide, in the *Paradiso*, the third and final part of the famous *Divine Comedy*. In Canto XXXIII, St. Bernard prays to Mary so that Dante's pilgrim might see the Eternal Light. Mary intercedes, and a smiling St. Bernard directs Dante's pilgrim to look up. The pilgrim does, and sees God, whom he describes as: "The Love which moves the sun and the other stars."[29]

St. Bernard was a useful guide in the non-heavenly spheres as well. In a letter to some of his fellow monks in a Swiss monastery in an alpine valley, St. Bernard described their chosen Cistercian life this way:

> Our place is lowliness, is humility, is voluntary poverty, and also obedience, peace, and joy in the Holy Spirit. Our custom is to live under a teacher, under an abbot, under the discipline of a rule. Our practice is to observe silence, to be generous in fasting, in early rising, praying and working with our hands. We strive especially to hold fast to the best way of all which is love. And furthermore, to advance day by day in all these practices, and to persevere in them until our final day.[30]

Some 700 years after the monastery at Cîteaux was built, Abbot Armand-Jean de Rance significantly reformed a Cistercian community in La Trappe in northern France. Thereafter, the Cistercians also commonly became known as "Trappists."[31]

My Trappist friends followed the sixth-century code of conduct established by St. Benedict, the European saint and father of monasticism, who also was the abbot of the large and famous fortress-like monastery at Monte Cassino in central Italy. St. Benedict's Rule is a "spiritual and practical guide for living the gospel," the "foundational text for Western Christian monasticism," and "marked by common sense."[32]

Many parts of the Rule are like a job description, a level-headed analysis of what may seem mundane or even obvious. For example, the Rule explains that a monk should not drink to excess, murmur, love sleep, be a glutton, or love boisterous laughter.[33] Other parts recite more lofty statements of mission and purpose, such as, "Whoever you are, if you wish to follow the path to God, make use of this little Rule for beginners.

Thus, at length you will come to the heights of doctrine and virtue under God's guidance."[34] Fortunately for me when I first started to visit the monastery, at least one part of the Rule, the one addressing the correction of youths, was not strictly enforced in the 1970s. This particular part states: "Every age and intelligence should be treated in a suitable manner. Youths who are at fault, or those who cannot understand the gravity of excommunication, shall receive just punishment (enforced fasting or flogging) so that they may be healed."[35]

A 1972 promotional brochure for the monastery, my first source of detailed information, explained that from "the beginning the orientation of Cistercian monasticism has been toward contemplative prayer, manual labor, and simplicity of life in a setting of solitude. Drawing inspiration from the Gospel and the Rules of St. Benedict, the first Cistercian monks desired to, 'prefer nothing to Christ.' (Rule, Ch. 4). The goal is the same today."[36]

The motherhouse of Holy Trinity Abbey was the Abbey of Gethsemani in Kentucky, the first Trappist monastery in the United States, founded in 1848.[37] In addition to sending forth the founders of Holy Trinity in 1947, Gethsemani also was home to Thomas Merton, the twentieth century's most famous American monk, writer, and mystic who died in 1968 of accidental electrocution.

Merton is known for several books, including a 1948 autobiography, *The Seven Storey Mountain*, which has sold millions of copies and been translated into many languages. Published at the end of World War II, Merton's book was great publicity for the Cistercians and probably encouraged many men to join the Trappist order. However, the monastic boom already was on even before Merton's book hit the presses.

A 2001 *New York Times* article explained how the existence of a monastery in Utah, in the heart of a valley dominated by Latter-day Saints, was due to the aftermath of World War II when returning Catholic soldiers flocked to Trappist abbeys.[38] A good example of this was one of first candidates to enter the Huntsville monastery: a large, strong, and quiet man from California called Brother Benedict, formerly known as Charles Philip Bernard Castro. Brother Benedict had been in the Army in World War II and suffered for a time in a German prisoner of war camp in Czechoslovakia.

The war likely guided him and other young men to monasteries for several reasons. As Georgia Trappist monk Matthew Torpey has explained, "You grow up pretty quick when people are dying around you and you might be the very next one. That's what brought them in, looking for some kind of meaning and some kind of meaning for what they had just been though."[39] However, this may not have been the only reason for the post-war monastic boom. "It was more than just the horrors of war. Many of the soldiers experienced great comradeship, and after the futility of war they wanted to do something positive with their lives."[40]

At its peak in the middle of the twentieth century, more than eighty men lived, worked and, most importantly, prayed at Holy Trinity Abbey.[41] Choosing to live in a monastery, monks value and seek out solitude, and in that sense are "cloistered." They rarely go places outside the abbey, but they are not strictly confined to monastery grounds as are members of other cloistered orders, such as Carmelite nuns. Father Casimir Bernas, who eventually served as an abbot at Holy Trinity, said, "It's a solitary life. We're not gloomy, but we're not engaged in a lot of backslapping either."[42] It also is a celibate life, but the choice is embraced and celebrated. As one Utah monk explained, "Celibacy does not leave us neutered beings, insensitive, self-centered, aloof, with a withered, shriveled affectivity. Our celibate monastic life creates in us a new and expanded heart, set free to love and be loved universally."[43]

According to Holy Trinity Abbey's old website, "As a contemplative, cloistered community we do not engage in Apostolic work outside our monastery. The monastic day consists of communal and private prayer, spiritual reading and courses in the sacred sciences, and productive labor on the farm or in small industries."[44] Their prayers were a gift to the world, an attempt to make the world a better place. "Monks share with all people of good will the ideal of renewing the face of the earth, but we work for the realization of that ideal in our own unique way, relying on the power of the Spirit of God who touches and transforms human hearts."[45]

Brother Boniface Ptasienski explained it this way: "We ask God to do what we cannot do. . . . I have nothing to do with the world. Yet, my influence is universal."[46] Another, Father David Kinney, told a news reporter, "We're here to pray. We're praying for the world and all the conditions in it. We're asking God to take care of it. Peace, peace,

peace. It's a calling. That's what a vocation is, a contemplative life devoted completely to God. It kind of helps, doesn't it, to know we are all up here praying for you?"[47]

I was about to find out.

■ ■ ■

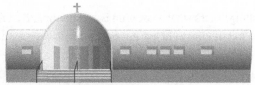

CHAPTER 6

First Friends

E‌very family has its own theology, its own concept of the divine, of ultimate meaning, of God, gods, or the lack of God, and of His or Her or Its essence, benevolence, demeanor, and nature. Such theologies serve as a base for the spiritual and cultural lives of the family members—a place of refuge and hope in difficult times, and a source of values and guiding principles in other times.

Family theologies evolve from a variety of sources, such as family tradition, culture, and history, affiliation or non-affiliation with institutional religion, politics, and everyday life-and-death experiences. These theologies may perfectly reflect an established doctrine or consist of a hodgepodge, or even mildly heretical collection, of various beliefs and practices. Family theologies also often develop in a nonlinear and unexpected manner. The O'Brien family theology is a case in point.

We were traditionally Catholic in many ways, and working-class, Irish Catholic at that. We had a solid record of service to the Church, with both nuns and priests in our family bloodline. We received all (or at least most) of the seven sacraments, starting with baptism and ending with the Sacrament of the Sick, which was called Extreme Unction back in the day. In between, there was First Confession, First Communion, Confirmation, and perhaps even marriage or Holy Orders (religious life). We went to catechism classes and Mass each week and attended extra Masses on Holy Days of Obligation.

In late winter, we went to school after early Ash Wednesday services and thereafter patiently responded, multiple times, to questions such as, "Did you know you have dirt on your forehead?" In early spring, we brought fresh palms home from Palm Sunday Mass and placed them on our mantle or behind picture frames, replacing the dried, yellowed and withered ones that had rested there for the past year. The Nativity scene was the first decoration we set out at Christmastime. We had to go to Easter midnight or morning Mass and sing "Jesus Christ has risen today, alllllleluia," before we could even think about diving into our Easter basket full of chocolate bunnies.

We also were Kennedy Catholics, another essential element of the family theology. Unlike my parents, I never have lived in a world where most Americans believed that a Catholic should not or could not possibly be president, or where prominent citizens actually verbalized the point and actively campaigned against someone because they thought he would take orders directly from the pope. John Fitzgerald Kennedy, not just a Catholic but an Irish Catholic, was a civic icon and cultural saint in our house, especially in those halcyon days before his personal indiscretions became more widely known.

One of my first childhood memories, either directly experienced or implanted, is of the day of JFK's assassination in November 1963, when I was almost three years old. Mom had been vacuuming the living room when CBS anchorman Walter Cronkite reported the awful news from Dallas on our black-and-white, General Electric television set. Mom immediately dropped the vacuum cleaner on the floor, where it remained untouched, next to the television that stayed on for most of the next five days, as the news of JFK's death and state funeral played out. Our house was enveloped in a wake-like atmosphere as if a close family member had died. An almost identical scene played out five years later when someone shot and killed JFK's brother, Senator Robert F. Kennedy, in California in June 1968. I remember watching television coverage of RFK's long funeral train ride from New York City to Washington, DC, when thousands gathered and stood solemnly by the side of the tracks to pay their respects during that last sad journey.

The house was somber and quiet too, just a few months earlier in April 1968, when American civil rights leader Martin Luther King Jr. was assassinated in Memphis. At age 7, I was confused about who had been shot. I asked my Mom, "Did a king die?" She said, "No, he was not a king. He was just a very good and kind man." Her comment reflected the Air Force in

1968, including the military housing where we lived, which was remarkably desegregated. Our neighbors in the adjoining home were Black. My mother drank coffee and smoked cigarettes with the mother of that family. They had a young son who was just another one of my neighborhood pals. When they got new military orders and had to move, my mom helped their mom clean their three-bedroom home. There were hugs and sad goodbyes. I did not really understand then that there were other American neighborhoods where such scenes did not play out the same way.

Although I never had thought of her as a scholar, it is clear to me now that part of our family theology developed because Mom was an avid reader of all books Catholic, especially after the divorce. Her library included traditionally orthodox teaching, such as the 1624 • *Heliotropium* by Jesuit Father Jeremias Drexelius; its opening lines summarize Christian doctrine as being "that man should absolutely and entirely conform himself to the Divine Will, in particulars as well as generals."[1] She also had more contemporary books, such as *Divorced Catholics.* That one described how she likely felt after her marriage ended, saying the "stigma of divorce for a Catholic" is like the shame of Hester Prynne in *The Scarlet Letter*—"a 'D' in the middle of their foreheads."[2]

Mom also owned books describing the lives of many of the saints (she favored St. Francis of Assisi and St. Thérèse of Lisieux—the "Little Flower"), and she had pamphlets about novenas and devotionals. One of her daily devotional books was based on the writings of Thomas Merton. She owned several books on faith and Catholic life authored by the New York bishop and Catholic television star Fulton J. Sheen. She also kept a yearly missal, a book that outlined numerous prayers and devotionals as well as all the Old and New Testament readings for daily Mass, which she attended several days each week.

Our popular cultural tastes also ran Catholic. We regularly watched Cecil B. De Mille's film *The Ten Commandments* and John Huston's movie called *The Bible: In the Beginning.* The family never missed a televised showing of the Catholic boarding school comedy movies *The Trouble with Angels* or *Where Angels Go, Trouble Follows.* We also watched *The Sound of Music* so many times that I can recite almost all the dialogue and sing all the songs from memory.

On the radio, we looked forward to hearing the Singing Nun (a former Dominican nun named Jeanne Decker) perform the hit "Dominique," in 1963, and to listen to Sister Janet Mead's 1974 hit "The Lord's Prayer." We also listened with mild disapproval (and some whispering and giggling) as Billy Joel bemoaned in the 1970s how "Catholic girls start much too late." Our television viewing regularly included Sally Field in *The Flying Nun*. Every Easter we tuned the television to watch *The Greatest Story Ever Told* with Max von Sydow as Jesus, and then, starting in 1977, to watch the miniseries *Jesus of Nazareth*, with Robert Powell in the lead and Anne Bancroft playing the role of Mary Magdalene.

Not every family favorite television broadcast, however, was faithfully Catholic. Indeed, I was stunned to come home from college one day to learn that Mom had become seriously addicted to *The Thorn Birds*, starring Richard Chamberlain and Rachel Ward and based on the novel by Colleen McCullough. The television miniseries told the story of Ralph de Briccasart, a young but ambitious Catholic priest and soon-to-be cardinal from Australia who constantly was grappling, often unsuccessfully, with the potent temptations of money, power, love, and sex. The priest eventually gave in to a lifelong passion for a younger woman, Meggie Cleary, whom he had known all of her life. Mom loved it! I asked her why she would enjoy a show involving a priest who broke every single one of his vows, including having sex with a woman fifteen years younger than he. She dismissed my skepticism, got a bit misty-eyed, and said, "Oh, but they really loved each other!"

Our family theology was unique in other ways, too, especially after the divorce. For a time, at St. Rose's Church in Layton, Mom dabbled in the Cursillo Movement, which originated in Spain.[3] While not widely known among Irish Catholics, it was popular at St. Rose's, which had a large Hispanic population. Mom went to a couple of Cursillo meetings with friends, some of whom claimed the gift of speaking in tongues, the language of the Holy Spirit. The whole concept of speaking in tongues confused me, because I thought we all used our tongues when we spoke.

I went to one meeting, too, and although I never got to hear anyone speaking in this strange new "tongues" language, I did leave with the indelible memory of the unofficial anthem of the movement, *"De Colores"* or "The Colors." The tune was addicting and the Spanish words wonderful,

referring to the colors of life all around us every day. A beautiful version
of the folk song, much like the one I first heard, is included in the 1989
movie *Romero*, starring Raul Julia, about the life and assassination of
St. Oscar Romero, the archbishop of El Salvador who spoke out against
repression in his country.[4]

Somewhat ironic for a Catholic girl who grew up during the pre-
Kennedy America that, at times, was outright hostile to her faith, Mom
also was a big fan of two of the most famous American Protestant
evangelical preachers of her time, Oral Roberts and Billy Graham. We
rarely missed *The Oral Roberts Show* on television on Sunday mornings,
usually singing along to his "God of Miracles" theme song about a
God reaching out to all of us miraculously. Perhaps missing the deeper
spiritual meaning of his messages, I was struck by how odd the first name
Oral was, and by how both he and his son Richard, who later took over
the ministry, had such big thick hair and big bright teeth.

Mom also loved the Billy Graham stadium crusades that were on
television in the 1970s. On occasion, I would watch part of them with her.
I think she found solace in his many positive messages, including about
how men and women need to find Jesus in their lives and that Jesus will
bring comfort to the afflicted soul. He was a great speaker, but my favorite
part of each program was when the great deep baritone voice of George
Beverly Shea led the choir in "How Great Thou Art," with his special
emphasis on hearing the rrrrooolllliiiiinnnngggg thunder. At the end of
each show, the choir sang the soft and sweet crusade theme song, the
1835 hymn "Just as I Am," while Graham beckoned all to come forward
and accept Jesus into their lives. The third verse, which laments being
tossed about and filled with doubt, always seemed especially relevant to
our family situation.

Although we watched the popular Protestant television preachers,
apparently we missed the famous local Utah Catholic television star,
Father Thomas Meersman. Father Meersman hosted a long-running TV
program and a radio program on Sunday mornings.[5] One day we were at
the Salt Lake Airport and ran into Catholic Bishop Joseph Lennox Federal.
We did not know him but approached him anyway and said hello. He
pointed to his traveling companion and said something like, "Of course,
you also know this man. . . ." Blank-faced, we sheepishly admitted we

did not. Bishop Federal said, "Well, don't you people watch television or listen to the radio on Sunday mornings?" He was with Father Meersman.

We soon would add classic Catholic monasticism to this eclectic family theology when we started to visit Holy Trinity Abbey more frequently. At first, I did not expect to interact all that much with the monks. I understood that monks did not abandon the outside world, but I certainly thought they rather firmly limited their active involvement with it. One of our friends from the abbey, Father David Altman, explains it better than me: "Monastic life is primarily an interior life of mind and heart, because there is so much aloneness with God."[6] As a result, like all new friendships, we eased our way into relationships there.

The bookstore was our first point of contact and there, in addition to Brother Felix, we also met Brother Boniface. He explained the monk's daily schedule to us:

- 3:15 a.m.: Rise
- 3:30 a.m.: Vigils (first hour of the monks' prayer sessions called the "Liturgy of the Hours")
- Breakfast
- Free time for reading, private prayer, or any personal interests
- 6:00 a.m.: Lauds (morning prayer)
- 6:20 a.m.: Mass
- 7:45 a.m.: Terce (service of the third hour of the monks' day)
- Work
- 12:15 p.m.: Sext (service of the sixth hour)
- Dinner
- Free time
- 2:15 p.m.: None (service of the ninth hour)
- Work or free time
- 5:30 p.m.: Vespers (evening prayer) and then Supper
- Free time
- 7:30 p.m.: Compline (in Latin, *completorium*, meaning prayers at the end of the day)
- Retire

The Sunday schedule allowed for more of a day of rest, with an additional public Mass later in the morning, occasionally also including a traditional Latin Mass.

Brother Boniface urged us to go listen to the monks' chant and pointed to a schedule for these services posted outside. Trappist monks' days are structured around what they call the "Liturgy of the Hours," a series of services set throughout the day and intended to facilitate, hour by hour, a closer relationship with God. Many of them are named roughly after the hour when celebrated, so "Terce" (roughly meaning the third hour of the day for the monks) was celebrated at 7:45 a.m., "Sext" (sixth hour) was celebrated at about noon and "None" (ninth hour) was celebrated at 2:15 p.m.[7]

As we looked at the schedule, we were there in time for "None," but we did not yet know the Trappist code, so we thought "None" meant, well, nothing, i.e. that there was no service at that particular time. There then unfolded a scene reminiscent of Abbott and Costello's comedy sketch "Who's on First?"

I asked, "Why would they would put 'None' on the list of services instead of just not mentioning a service at all?"

My sister Karen helpfully suggested, "Maybe there used to be a service at that time that had been discontinued, and so they put 'None' on the schedule so people would know there was not a service anymore."

Our discussion dragged on and I think we missed that first chance to attend "None," but eventually we figured it out.

Another good example of our ignorance of the monk code is what I call the "snow Mass" incident. We heard the monks refer a number of times to a "snow Mass." I assumed this was something like a folk Mass, only said outdoors and in bad weather. My preteen brain imagined a priest in boots and parka, a frozen altar, the offertory gifts arriving on skis, and shivering but loyal worshipers in the congregation. I must not have been the only one confused, because one day my sister Karen asked one of the monks about the snow Mass. At first, he looked confused, but then he smiled and suggested that what we had heard was a reference to "Snowmass," i.e., the nickname for St. Benedict's Monastery, another Trappist community high in the Rocky Mountains in Snowmass, an unincorporated community in Colorado.[8]

Speaking of Mass, one day someone told us the monks offered a midday Sunday Mass that was later (and easier for us non-monks to get to) than their usual daily Mass starting at 6:20 a.m. We decided to check it out. After our long but scenic drive from Clearfield, we expected to see a traditional and serious Gregorian-like service with incense and candles and the hooded monks chanting in their choir stalls in the main chapel. This preconception shows how little we knew about monks, or how we had a rather stereotypical view of how monks prayed, but also how we expected to be passive observers at the monastery rather than active participants in the lives of the monks. We could not have been more wrong. When we arrived, we were surprised to find an altar set up outside on the lawn and a collection of guitars and other instruments. It was a folk Mass, such a typical seventies thing to do!

I have not conducted any detailed scholarly or historical research on liturgies at Trappist monasteries throughout the world, but I doubt that a folk Mass is a usual offering at many of them. Yet, it was at Holy Trinity Abbey in the summer of 1972, and we went to almost all of them. These summer folk Masses helped to jump-start the close relationship with the monks that we later developed.

Not all the monks attended the folk Mass, but many did. Two new members of the community, Brother Jonathan Cloud (a postulant) and Brother Gregory Allard (a novice), provided youthful energy to the group, along with Brother Isidore Sullivan, a vigorous and charismatic man whose favorite adjective for everything was "strong." The lovely voices of Brother Carl Holton or Father Alan Hohl led the singing. Father Alan, in addition to his work managing the abbey's farm operations, was also the cantor, or lead singer, for the monastery choir. Brother Carl seemed to be the assistant cantor.

The first monk we met, Brother Felix, who also loved to sing (but tended to do so off key), was there from time to time too. Various Trappist monk-priests led the Masses on a rotating basis, and we soon learned their names: Father Patrick Boyle, Father Virgil Dusbabek, Father Andrew Marek, Father Bartholomew Gottemoller, and Father Charles Cummings. Brother Boniface floated in and out of the picture, and we also met another monk, Brother (soon to be Father) David Altman. Taking in the whole folk Mass scene with a big grin on his face and a

tambourine in his hand was none other than the abbot himself, the Right
Rev. Dom Emmanuel Spillane. According to the Rule of St. Benedict, the
abbot has absolute power in a monastery, is to be obeyed, and answers to
God for his arbitrary or unjust acts.[9] In the Catholic leadership hierarchy,
an abbot is on par with a bishop.

Known to his family as Joseph J. Spillane ("Joe") and eventually to us
as Father Manny, he came to the monastery early in 1950 after serving
as a priest in the Archdiocese of Los Angeles, California. He was born in
New York City, with ancestors from County Cork in Ireland, but he grew
up in Southern California as one of two sons of a family of actors. He
dabbled in the theater himself for a few years before deciding to become
a priest. He served Catholics in the ritzy Hollywood church of St. Basil's,
on Wilshire Boulevard, and between his assignment and his acting, was
friends with many of the film and theater stars of the day. At age 33, after
working as a parish priest for five years, he decided to join the monastery.

His choice generated headlines in both the *Los Angeles Times* and the
Ogden Standard-Examiner, which described him as a "Hollywood priest."
He told reporters, "I feel that I can do more through a life of penance and
prayer than I have done in the outside world."[10] His decision must have
been a matter of providence, because the Utah monks elected him as their
abbot in 1956 at age thirty-nine, shortly after the founding Abbot Lans
died, and replacing temporary superior Father Bellarmine McQuiston.
Father Manny served in that role for about twenty-six years. He was a big
and solid man, also a former football player, and larger than life. He had
a shiny bald head, a round face, a solid jaw, a warm personality, a deep
voice, and a loud laugh. Someone, perhaps Father Manny himself, once
told us he was related to the famous crime novelist Mickey Spillane.[11]

He managed simultaneously to exude a deep and traditional monastic
spirituality and a sort of California cool. One year we helped him address
his Christmas cards. His mailing list included family members, bishops,
and archbishops, Hollywood actors, famous singers, and even professional
football players, such as his niece's husband Bob Klein, who played for the
NFL's Los Angeles Rams until 1976. One of Father Manny's former monk
colleagues, a possible detractor, nonetheless has described the abbot's
decision to leave his glittery ministry in California as "a heroic decision—
motivated consciously by idealistic spiritual striving."[12] Thomas Merton

liked him, too, when they interacted at a Trappist leadership meeting in October 1964.[13]

As the monastery's abbot, Father Manny once joined several other Cistercian leaders in meeting the pope. A few years after this papal audience, we had an interesting, but somewhat confusing, discussion with him about the election of a new pope. In August 1978, Pope Paul VI died, and the College of Cardinals replaced him with Italian Cardinal Albino Luciani, Pope John Paul I, who served for only a month before his unexpected death. The cardinals then gathered again in October 1978 for a second papal conclave in just three months. The year 1978 would be one of the rare years with three popes.

We happened to see Father Manny, and I asked him, "Who do you think will be the next pope?" He told us (Mom and Karen were there, too), "I am praying for Cardinal Sin." We nodded politely and smiled, and he left. My sister said, "Is he joking? Isn't a cardinal sin a bad thing, like one of the seven deadly sins?" But I continued my research and soon figured out that Father Manny actually was referring to Cardinal Jaime Sin of the Philippines.

A week later, I was sitting in a high school class during the afternoon of October 16, 1978, when the loudspeaker came on and our student body president Shawn Mario Alfonsi announced that the new pope was not Cardinal Sin, but rather Cardinal Karol Wojtyla. Shawn could not quite pronounce "Wojtyla" and so, like any good Italian would do, he gave it a Venetian spin and said something that sounded like "Vontolli." He then also announced that the new pope was from Poland, causing our English teacher, Dolores Obuszewski, of proud Polish heritage, to squeal with delight.

I went home that afternoon to watch the new pope's first appearance on the balcony of St. Peter's Basilica. We had an ancient, black-and-white television with a rabbit-ears antenna. Once we got the antenna perfectly placed and the room nearly totally dark, we finally were able to see on the screen a fuzzy outline of the new pope giving his first papal blessing. Although his predecessor served for only about thirty days, Pope John Paul II served the Church for almost thirty years.

I am certain that Father Manny was the main reason there were folk Masses at Holy Trinity when we first started visiting there in the summer of 1972. He loved them and loved to be a part of them. He likely is one of the few superiors of a religious order who managed to stay in office both before and after the many dramatic changes that came with the Second Vatican Council in the early 1960s. Any doubts that he loved the folk Masses were erased simply by watching the way he played his musical instrument of choice—the tambourine—during the Eucharistic celebrations.

I remember one song in particular, called the "Song of Good News" by Father Willard Jabusch.[14] It had a traditional Israeli melody and started rather slowly and methodically, telling Christians to open their hearts to the good news of the gospel. The tempo increased dramatically on the chorus, explaining how God speaks to the people. Suddenly, it was tambourine time for Father Manny. During each such chorus, the tambourine in his hand virtually exploded with movement and with sound. I am surprised he never broke it. He played that instrument with an energy and vigor I had never seen before and may never see again. And he grinned the whole time.

It was amazing and startling to see a man so easily and comfortably walk in two different realms, the world of traditional, even ancient, monasticism and the more modern universe of the twentieth century. Just a few hours after standing in the sunshine wearing aviator sunglasses while playing his tambourine along with various folk melodies, he could walk with quiet dignity and propriety into the simple beauty of the abbey's chapel and chant ancient songs in the Gregorian style. Speaking to his fellow monks at Mass, Father Manny would expound on Christian Scriptures, but then also remind them that a Hindu leader from India named Mahatma Gandhi had once accurately remarked that more persons would be Christian if more Christians were Christlike. Continuing a longstanding practice from the early Church, he could solemnly hold a chain and censer, bearing the sweet-smelling incense of traditional Latin Catholicism, and ritualistically swing it to venerate the Blessed Sacrament. Yet, a moment later, he also could (and frequently did) freely quote from modern American poetry.

His favorite modern poem was "Balloons Belong in Church," written by Presbyterian poet Ann Weems. Fr. Manny brought balloons to Mass one day and read the poem. He said it was written when the poet's young son brought a bright balloon to Sunday services, helping Weems understand that church is a joyful celebration. In the poem, Weems asks why we ever thought balloons did not belong in church. Fr. Manny responded to her question by blowing up a dozen of them and inviting God and the rest of us to his church party. Emmanuel means "God is with us." Fr. Manny bore that name well.[15]

During one 1972 folk Mass, I got sick to my stomach. Brother Jonathan Cloud and Brother Gregory Allard helped my sister and me to the nearby guesthouse. They got me a Sprite to drink—the oft-prescribed O'Brien family elixir for digestive woes. I got to rest in the luxurious (by Holy Trinity standards) Bishop's Suite. After that, we managed to talk with the two of them almost every time we were there. They became good friends with Mom and my sister and me.

Brother Gregory, from Billings, Montana, was magnetic. His face, and especially his prominent forehead, glowed red with excitement and a zest for life. He laughed quickly and loudly. He was a novice, meaning he had been at the monastery for only a year or two and had taken simple, but not final vows. He also was the artist who designed the monastery brochure. Brother Jonathan was slightly taller and lankier than Brother Gregory and was just a postulant, meaning he had been there only a few months. He was far from home, having grown up in Maine. He had curly brown hair and wore a full beard. He was quiet and more introspective than Brother Gregory, but he also was quite friendly and had a kind and gentle smile.

We came to know them as Jonathan and Gregory, and even referred to them without the title "Brother" when they were not around. Every time we went to the monastery, I hoped we would see them. Sometimes I think they even may have snuck out just to see us. I did not realize this until later, but I am sure they were both quite young themselves (likely no older than their middle or late twenties) and they probably were seriously searching for meaning and direction in their own lives.

I was sad when they both, at different times and on cold days, told us they were leaving the monastery to continue their life searches elsewhere. I never saw Jonathan again, but he said he was leaving because he wanted to have a wife and children. I stayed in touch with Gregory for a while and was lucky to visit him a decade later when I was in college at Notre

Dame and he was teaching special education classes at an urban school in Detroit. I do not know what eventually became of either one of them, but they were funny and cool, and I remember them with great affection.

In 1972, they took me behind the scenes, past the gates of the monastery, on a little tour. I had a real advantage over my Mom and sister, because women were not allowed behind those gates. I felt special and privileged. Jonathan and Gregory told me how such a tour would not have been possible in past years, when the monks used to remain silent nearly always. While some might look upon this as a burden, being quiet is an essential element of a prayerful life of solitude. Yet, it apparently also served a more practical purpose. Thomas Merton once humorously explained how the Kentucky retreat master attributed monastic cordiality to the rule of silence, given that the abbey was a "mixture of men." The old monk suggested to Merton that in a house full of "lawyers and farmers and soldiers and schoolboys . . . It's a good thing they don't talk."[16]

When total silence was the rule, the monks would communicate through a special sign language, but sometimes the silence rule trumped even the sign language option. One Utah monk recalled the story of how at Gethsemani Abbey in Kentucky a major building on the grounds caught fire in the middle of the night. The building was a total loss because the one monk who woke up would not speak to warn anyone, despite seeing the flames.[17] This silence rule has been relaxed over time at Trappist monasteries everywhere. Eventually the monks talked during the day and observed what they rather lyrically called "the Great Silence" from about 8 p.m. at night to around 3:30 a.m. the next day.[18]

Continuing my tour, Jonathan and Gregory took me to see the abbey's high-tech award-winning dairy, run by Father Joseph Schroer. Father Joseph was a kind, gentle, hardworking man who looked like he was going to die from acute embarrassed shyness whenever you made eye contact with him. The monastery had several dozen dairy cows. Most of the monks arose at 3:15 a.m., but Father Joseph was in the dairy by 2 a.m. because the cows had to be milked twice a day, morning and afternoon on the twos. During the harsh Huntsville winters, the cows themselves provided the only heat in the dairy.

I doubt that there ever was a group of dairy animals so lovingly cared for and tended to. Father Joseph served as a sort of bovine midwife for the dairy, personally delivering into the world sixty or seventy calves during his many years managing the herd, likely including all of the cows I saw on my tour.[19] He would leave his bedroom in the middle of the night to check on his expectant mothers. An accomplished electrician, he eventually rigged up a closed-circuit television system so he could keep an eye on them from his office. Father Joseph also named each of his cows, for example calling them Wilma, Josie, Luella, Star, and Sippy.

No trip to the dairy was complete without a visit to the nursery, where I met several new arrivals. Jonathan convinced me to put my fingers near one newborn calf's mouth. Quickly, the calf was suckling on my fingers and growing a bit annoyed that no mother's milk flowed from them. I was not as attracted to the fresh farm milk as were the calves. I tried it on several occasions, and it had a strong and somewhat pungent and unpleasant taste. The monks must have known this, and they often anticipated and hospitably eased my drinking discomfort by bringing along hot cocoa mix whenever they served us their milk.

My tour also included a walk past some of the abbey's wheat and barley fields, all named after saints, and its cattle herd, several hundred head strong. We toured the bullpen, containing a live and large bull, with what seemed to be very large and very sharp horns. Jonathan and Gregory told me the story of how a few years before, one of the monks was playfully using his belt to tease a similar 2,600-pound Holstein bull in the same pen. The belt somehow got stuck on the bull's horn and fell into the pen after the bull jerked his head in response to the teasing. The good but naïve brother climbed over the fence and into the pen to retrieve his belt, but as he turned to leave, the bull suddenly gored him. He did not survive the incident and became one of the initial occupants of the small cemetery adjoining the church. I never had much interest in wearing a belt after hearing that story.

Leaving the farm area, Jonathan and Gregory also gave me a good look at the monastery building itself. It was rectangular, with a lawn and courtyard in the middle. The Quonset structure was architecturally unique, as most Trappist and other monasteries are constructed of brick or stone.[20] Inside the church, we stopped to admire the raised altar, set serenely in the front, before what indisputably was the most spectacular and memorable feature of the church, the Salve window.

Salve is short for "Salve Regina" or "Hail Holy Queen," a traditional Catholic song of praise for Mary, the Mother of Jesus. The original was clear glass. One morning in about 1955 while the monks were at prayer, an epic storm blew through and shattered the window, causing the monks to scramble for shelter to avoid flying shards. The monks boarded up the window with wood for several years afterward, then finally replaced it in the 1960s with beautiful, stained glass panels meticulously designed by the artist George D. Merrill. The exquisite nine-foot-wide window dedicated to Mary, the patroness of the monastery, dominated the eastern wall, rising some twenty-one feet, most of the full height of the church.

My new monk friends explained how the window's breathtaking eighteen panels presented an ancient story. Mary, seeming to levitate in the center, wore a white veil, a golden crown, and a green-and-gold robe trimmed in red-and-blue diamonds. Her right hand was raised as a greeting (after all, the Latin *salve* means "hello"), and perhaps also in a gesture calling for silence in the tradition of gestures used by Roman orators.[21] Her bare left foot stood firmly on a coiled gray snake, causing the serpent's red tongue to hiss in obvious discontent. Mary's left arm lovingly cradled her young child, Jesus. With a slight smile on her face, Mary's haloed head tilted just to her right as her eyes gently, but protectively, gazed upon her much-loved son.

The beneficiary of this unmistakable and unconditional maternal adoration and devotion, the young Jesus she held, wore a red robe with royal-purple trim, and also was crowned in gold and a halo. A turquoise aura embellished with white stars swirled behind both their heads, a kind of cosmos connection. Jesus was barefoot, too, and held a bright-blue orb in his left hand. Like that of his blessed mother, his right hand was raised, with thumb, index, and middle fingers also pointing toward heaven.

The window's background, behind and to the sides of Jesus and Mary, was a lively sea of a half-dozen shades of blue. Red branches bolted out in all directions from the mother and child, perhaps symbolic of divine love emanating to the surrounding universe and all who occupy it. In darkness, a soft, white light highlighted the window's attractive features. It was at its most resplendent in the early morning as the rising sun illuminated it from behind and caused reflected light to dance on the chapel's whitewashed walls, wooden altar, and surrounding tile floors.[22]

Leaving the church, my guides continued as we walked into the living quarters of the monastery. I discovered that the monks used to sleep in a common dormitory room, in their own cubicles, on hard straw mattresses. This evolved into an arrangement where they had individual rooms or cells, furnished sparsely with a bed, desk, chair, lamp, and crucifix. I visited the laundry, business offices, and a couple of classrooms. I also saw the refectory and large tables where the monks ate their meals together, their seat determined by their seniority. Each had his own place, including a name tag, set plate, napkin, and what looked like an army-issued tin cup.

The monks made their monastic clothes on site and wore them year-round. Early photos show that initially, while at work, certain brothers wore coarse brown or blue robes. In winter, in addition to a standard white robe covered with a black-hooded scapular (a form of apron), they wore a white cowl that completely covered them. The cowl sleeves were long, said to be symbolic of service, i.e., that the monks really had no hands of their own but were left in God's hands and God's care. Like most everything else in their lives, the mandatory brown or black leather belt, called a "cincture," was a symbol that each man was bound to God and listened to hear God's voice in all things.[23]

I also toured the adjoining industrial-sized kitchen where the monks prepared and cooked their food. It was the largest and best-equipped kitchen I had ever seen and probably rivaled the meal preparation spaces of fine commercial restaurants. Jonathan and Gregory explained how the monks were vegetarians by choice, but on special occasions (such as the abbey's twenty-fifth anniversary in July 1972) they ate hamburgers or Kentucky Fried chicken. Father Patrick Boyle from the monastery once told a news reporter, "How could any American live without hamburgers?" Over the years, they added more protein to their everyday diets, primarily eggs and cheese.[24]

From the kitchen we walked to the industrial-sized bakery, where they baked the monastery's famous wheat bread. The bread was a deep auburn-brown color and smelled and tasted of honey. It also was substantial; just one slice could fill you up. I loved that bread, especially the crusts, and particularly when it was still hot. The monks stopped baking it several years before the monastery closed, but anyone now can make it at home because the monks published the recipe. In addition to appearing on the monastery's website,[25] the bread is so well known and popular that the recipe is available at Food.com.[26]

Nothing goes better with monk bread than monk honey. Two famous Catholics—Eileen Egan and Dorothy Day—have confirmed it. Egan was a New York Catholic writer and activist who was friends with Mother Teresa of Calcutta and wrote several books about her. Day, of course, founded the Catholic Worker Movement and was an activist for the poor. Pope Francis, in his 2015 speech to the United States Congress, stated that Day's "passion for justice and for the cause of the oppressed, were inspired by the Gospel, her faith, and the example of the saints."[27] In 1978, Egan visited the Utah monastery and sent Trappist bread and honey to Day. Day thought enough of the gift to note it in her newspaper, *The Catholic Worker*:

> Eileen Egan sent out home-made bread and creamed honey from Holy Trinity Abbey, Huntsville, Utah. She had been attending a meeting of co-workers of Mother Teresa of India nearby — and the Abbot of Holy Trinity had remembered my visit there. The monks sent promises of prayers. Since our beginnings in the Thirties, Trappists have been close to us, and we depend on their prayers.[28]

I toured the rooms where the monastery made its famous flavored creamed honey. The resident beekeeper was Father Bartholomew Gottemoller, another one of the original monks from Gethsemani Abbey. A monastery pamphlet asked the mouthwatering question, "How do we make Trappist creamed honey?" The very tasteful answer was:

> The alfalfa-clover honey is carefully mixed with choice nut meats, fruit pieces, flavored extracts, or fresh spices. Each of the different flavors is allowed to age until it has naturally changed to a fine, crystalline state, giving it a soft, creamy texture that is delicious on fresh bread or toast.[29]

I saw photos of Father Bartholomew tending the bees while wearing his beekeeper spacesuit. Although often stung (including once inside his nose), he was a big fan of the hive dwellers, saying, "It's amazing what bees can do," and calling them "a revelation of God."[30] I never knew, until much later, that Father Bartholomew also was a famous and prolific writer of scholarly books and articles on theology and spirituality, and he had served as a mentor for Thomas Merton when Merton entered Gethsemani. He also was a good plumber. He was as busy as his bees.

Some of the rooms used for the honey-processing operations also served as a civil defense nuclear fallout shelter, a sign of the Cold War mutual assured destruction era that dominated the world in the 1970s. The abbey had been licensed by the government as a shelter in 1967. Father Bartholomew explained the dual purposes of his honey rooms: "God wants us to live as he destines us, and he wants us to take all the precautions we can to preserve life."[31] The monks fulfilled their civic duties in other ways, too. Beginning in the 1970s, they voted regularly at their assigned Huntsville precinct. A wonderful 1980 newspaper photo shows Brother Boniface, Brother Felix, Father Thomas, and Father Bartholomew voting. Brother Felix is waving his ballot in the air for the camera. The photo caption reports, "The brothers kept silent on their ballot choices."[32]

My personal tour continued along to the infirmary, where I met Father Brendan Hanratty, the infirmarian who took care of the old and sick monks. This must have been a big job because even then, the monastery's population was aging. Father Brendan had a twinkle in his eye, spoke with a slight Irish brogue, and wore a great salt-and-pepper goatee-like beard. He was from Crossmaglen, County Armagh, came to America in 1928, and served in the Army as an optician. He was assigned to the Pacific forces in World War II. He saw fierce battles and was "so dismayed with the needless loss of life in that particularly bloody conflict that he immediately joined the Trappist Order."[33] In his spare time at the monastery, he also served as the prior, or second in command after Father Manny.

What Jonathan and Gregory showed me was an amazing, largely self-sufficient and sustainable community. The abbey certainly had available to it a variety of skills attained by its residents before and after they became monks. Many were accomplished scholars and writers in theology, history, and various languages, including Latin and French.

For example, Father Casimir Bernas, who joined at 19, studied to be a priest and received a licentiate (master's degree) in Theology from the Angelicum University in Rome, and then a licentiate in Sacred Scripture from the Pontifical Biblical Institute in Rome. Finally, he earned a doctorate in Sacred Scripture from the Pontifical Biblical Institute. He wrote his doctoral dissertation about the Jewish festival of Yom Kippur (the Day of Atonement) in New Testament times. He did much of his research work from the monastery's well-stocked library.

On a more practical level, Brother Boniface was a chemist who served in Europe in the Army during World War II, as did Father Brendan. Brother Felix worked for the Civilian Conservation Corps. Father David was an accountant. Father Joseph was an electrician. Brother Bonaventure Schweiger was an engineer, a trained chef, and a skilled mechanic, and had served in the Korean War. Brother Cyril Anderson survived the World War II battle at Iwo Jima. Brother Mark Stazinski was a Navy veteran of World War II and an accomplished carpenter and cook. Father Andrew Marek was an expert in finances and investments. Brother Carl Holton had a master's degree in forestry.[34]

The abbey even had its own naturalists, including an amateur meteorologist and a wildlife expert. The US government once cited Brother Felix for his diligent and detailed day-by day recordings of many years of Ogden Valley weather.[35] A 1965 outdoors column in the *Ogden Standard-Examiner* outlined the vast knowledge about Mother Nature that Brother George Yungwirth had acquired just by keeping a keen eye on the monastery's property. Brother George had spent hours observing such animals as elk, deer, gophers, ground squirrels, mountain lions, game birds, rabbits, skunks, porcupines, and mink.[36] Apparently, Brother George and some of the other monks even captured and tried to tame a female bobcat. However, the newspaper reported that the cat was "a bit old for such antics," and as a result, did not cooperate and "never really became a friend to anyone."[37]

As a preteen, mostly urban kid, I thought it all was so interesting. As with most valuable lessons of life, I probably did not fully appreciate it then, but now I marvel at how well the monastery appeared to run and how effectively and efficiently three dozen monks tended to such a detailed and expansive operation and cared for each other. It was an early version of the sustainable sharing economy that has been so popular and much discussed in the first few decades of the twenty-first century. As Thomas Merton has described it, "The life of each one in this abbey is part of a mystery. We all add up to something far beyond ourselves."[38]

When they were not giving me tours or letting me pretend to help them work on the farm, Jonathan and Gregory would just walk and talk with us. There was a wonderful road for such strolling. As a Beatles fan, I like to call it Abbey Road. It curved and meandered for about a half a mile or so from the entrance gate to the main building and farmhouses. Part of the road was lined with maples, elms, and pines. The part that was not tree-lined abutted the pastureland, with sweeping vistas and spectacular views of Mount Ogden and the valley below. I must have walked Abbey Road over a hundred times either with my family or with various monks, and sometimes alone.

One walk was particularly memorable. Mom and Karen and I were strolling and talking with Jonathan and Gregory. By now, we were getting to know them quite well. One of them commented how the white monastic robes they wore were much more comfortable in the summer even than wearing pants. It must have been our increased comfort level with them that provoked my sister Karen to ask, "What do you wear under there?" Jonathan and Gregory looked at each other, smiled, and without saying a word, simultaneously hiked their robes up just above the knee line to display four hairy legs. Karen blushed. Mom was shocked and speechless.

I thought it was hilarious. *I might not mind*, I told myself, *spending more time with these unusual men who call themselves monks.*

CHAPTER 7

Brother Good Face

D URING THE FIRST YEARS OF MY MONASTERY MORNINGS, a boy's social status and number of friends often depended on his school playground proficiency. Compared to most of my classmates, I was mired in a small preadolescent body incapable of producing hair anywhere except on the top of my head. This proved to be an extreme disadvantage as I struggled to be seen and fought for a place in the male pecking order.

I stood four foot something, weighed less than your average ninety-pound weakling, and did not get my growth spurt until high school. Despite my size, I was dogged, a puny Chihuahua with delusions of bulldog or greyhound grandeur. The biggest thing about me was my outsized competitive urge, which had no business dwelling in a chassis that only rarely could satisfy its revved-up demands. I told myself that energy, enthusiasm, and sheer force of will could compensate for lack of size, speed, and strength. My classmates rarely agreed. I was the last man standing when we picked sides for football teams.

We were living in Ogden, and I attended St. Joseph's Catholic Grade School, which sat on the corner of Lincoln Avenue and 28th Street. Our little corner of Ogden's rough and tumble West Side was just steps away from the notorious 25th Street, nicknamed "Two Bit Street." It was a place, apparently, that even gangster Al Capone said was too wild for his tastes. Our two-story school building, dedicated in 1923 during the height of the Prohibition Era, was constructed using an odd-colored brick, too dark to be brown but not quite black, so I just call it "brack."[1]

When I attended there, the fifty-year-old school was surrounded by deteriorating houses and nondescript industrial plants. The area immediately around the school was an urban asphalt jungle consisting of grassless, paved, and painted playing fields, as well as concrete sports courts. It was on those hardened surfaces that I worked relentlessly, day after day, to change minds and reveal the big dog no one else could see. One day, fate lent me a hand. While I was playing defense in a touch football game, an errant pass came my way. I caught it and started my return of the prized interception. The only plausible return path was one we all usually avoided, the dreaded north sideline. This boundary of our asphalt "field" was an extensive patch of a weed commonly called "puncturevine." The plant's name could not be more appropriate. Its vines produce a "fruit" (seed containers called goatheads), a small pod with sharp spines that readily pierce whatever they happen to touch—clothes, shoe, skin. The weed's official botanical name, *Tribulus Terrestris*, means the "tribulation on the earth."[2]

No such earthly tribulation, however, was going to block me from grasping the playground pick six glory beckoning to me when I intercepted the football. I ran for the sideline route and was approaching the goal line when the opposing team's quarterback, the boy who had thrown the interception, landed an assertive two-hand-touch on my lower back, with just a bit of extra push for emphasis. I lost my footing, went airborne, and scored a touchdown by landing on my right side, in bounds, but in puncturevine overgrowth.

It seemed like a defining boyhood athletic moment, one destined to change the perceptions of my fellow schoolyard athletes. Nothing ever hurt quite so good. The next day at school I still was nursing my wounds, with numerous red welts where the various puncturevine stickers had stuck. Yet, I strode confidently onto the asphalt field at lunch recess, ready for another game, and where possible, coyly displaying the puncturevine badges of glory on my right side and arm. Two new team captains were chosen, and they drafted their players for the day. I was chosen last, again. Again!

My puncturevine wounds eventually healed, and as the array of tiny red marks slowly but steadily disappeared, the physical discomfort they caused dissipated too. Another form of boyhood misery persisted. The pain of being overlooked is an invisible but deep wound. I longed for someone to notice me, to see me. Someone did. I met him on the first day we visited Holy Trinity Abbey, on the same day that we met Brother Felix. Although we spent more time talking with Brother Felix that day, near the end of our first visit we spoke briefly with Brother Boniface too, who also was working in the bookstore. As we left the store, I asked him to tell us his last name. A wisecracking Brother Felix suggested that he better write it down. He did . . . P-t-a-s-i-e-n-s-k-i.

His full given name was Mieczyslaw (Milton) Anthony Ptasienski, the Polish son of an immigrant laborer named Adalbert Ptasienski and his wife Janina Bejgrowicz, and a native of the Bronx. He was an avid Yankees fan. Despite a roster that included legendary names like Ruth and Gehrig, Milton's favorite player was all-star Bill Dickey, the Yankee catcher for almost twenty years while Milton was growing up.

Milton Ptasienski was a devout Catholic and a true New Yorker. His sister became a nun, joining the Felician order in Connecticut. It took Milton a little longer to take the same path, in part because he had a sharp wit and tongue. He once told me, with fond recollection, how he had ordered a ham sandwich from an overly thrifty deli worker. While watching the deli worker make the sandwich, Milton smiled and told him, "Mister, if you slice that ham any thinner, you will miss it altogether." He attended Catholic schools in New York and New Jersey, including Don Bosco High School, where he played for the basketball team that won both the New Jersey State championship and the Catholic League championship. He later told a classmate that his time at Don Bosco was his "second Baptism." After graduating in 1937, he enrolled in Jesuit-run Fordham University and earned a chemistry degree.

In college, he joined the ROTC program and later served in the Army for four years, earning the rank of Staff Sergeant as a photo-interpreter and linguist. The Army paid for him to attend Harvard University to learn Russian (he already was fluent in Polish), which he later used in military intelligence operations. With his training, he worked with generals in charge of famous battles like the 1944–45 Battle of the Bulge. He earned two bronze stars serving in Europe during the most intensive and climactic years of World War II.[3]

As was true for many other young men of his era, what Milton saw in war, during the final years of Hitler's now-devastated Europe, set him on an intensive search for peace, a quest to answer what he described as "this deep call in my heart of work and prayer."[4] Answering this call, he soon arrived at Gethsemani Abbey, still wearing his Army uniform, and entered the Cistercian order. He likely felt, as did Thomas Merton (who joined just before Milton), that he "was enclosed in the four walls of my new freedom."[5] Just a few years later, while still a novice, he was one of the youngest of the three dozen monks sent west on a train to start a new monastery in Utah.

The Depression-era Bronx neighborhood where Milton grew up was diverse both ethnically and culturally, a place where Irish and Italian bootleggers roamed mean streets while immigrant families tried to forge homes in rough tenement flats. Once in Utah, this urban man could not help noticing the stark contrasts between his boyhood abode and his monastic home. "I was surprised to find myself out here in these canyons of the Rocky Mountains when I lived in the canyons of New York City with tall buildings."[6] In 1951, four years after he arrived out West, Milton, now as Brother Boniface, made his final vows and promised to stay at Holy Trinity Abbey for the rest of his life. He did, and viewed his promise as significant. He once told a news reporter about a visitor who had arrived at the abbey thinking the monks were "weak men hiding from society," but left the place admiring "the manliness of their commitment."[7]

Brother Boniface humbly served in many roles. An anonymous journal written by one of the pioneer monks who traveled from Kentucky to Huntsville with him indicates that, in addition to construction laborer and ditch digger, the first job Brother Boniface had in Utah was to milk the new abbey's thirty cows, using a four-unit, electric milker.[8] Over the years, he worked as assistant director of novices, baker, tailor, porter, farm irrigation specialist, bookstore manager, and supervisor of the egg production business. He also served as a spiritual advisor and inspiration for countless abbey visitors—people like me.

Some of the most interesting insights about Brother Boniface are in his own personal daily missal prayer booklet, which I was able to read years after I first knew him. The timeworn missal, which he used for almost three decades, is a liturgical book containing daily Mass texts,

Bible readings, and various other devotionals. He used it as a tool for prayer, meditation, and spiritual growth, and heavily annotated it with his thoughts, petitions, and worshipful praises.[9] His entries were written in English, Latin, Polish, and occasionally even in Spanish and Greek. He quoted from a number of biblical writers, as well as from theologian Karl Rahner, German philosopher Immanuel Kant, Polish-American Rabbi A. J. Heschel, French Jesuit Teilhard de Chardin, Mother Teresa of Calcutta, Pope Paul VI, and his beloved fellow Pole, Pope John Paul II. He even attributed one inspirational quote to the American tractor maker John Deere: "There are no easy solutions, only intelligent choices."

We tend to think of monks as settled and secure in their spiritual life. Consistent with that conventional wisdom, Brother Boniface's notes repeated a half-dozen words or phrases, a sort of sacred shorthand slogans he used to express his abiding faith and utter devotion to God. On dozens of pages he wrote "*Deo Gratias*," a simple Latin thank you to God. He often indicated the time of day when he wrote it, typically in the predawn hours when monks supplicate while the rest of us slumber. Brother Boniface regularly invited Jesus into his heart when he scribbled the formal Latin word "*veni*," meaning "come." He admonished his heart and mind to be open to the word of God when he often wrote the Latin word "*ausculta*," which means to "give ear" or listen. He liked to write "*fiat*" (Latin for "let it be done") by prayers or readings about the will of God. Throughout the book, he recalled his Polish roots and used the Polish language of his parents when he wrote "*waira*," meaning "faith" and "belief."

Yet, perhaps unexpectedly, Brother Boniface's writings also confirm that he, like the rest of us, had his share of human doubts and struggles. Some pages are left completely blank, as if his earnest but exhausted soul had nothing to say on the day he encountered those parts of his missal. On one page he lamented, "Help me in my unbelief." On another, he acknowledged his personal failures, and the difficulties of his vocation, with the candid admission, "keep trying!" And try he did. He composed, in all caps, what seems to be a mantra designed to help him pass through moments of doubt or temptation: "VOWS MONASTERY PERSEVERANCE." Facing down his doubts, he appealed to the patroness of the abbey and wrote, "Ave Maria…In silence and trust shall be your strength." He comforted himself with soothing reminders such as: "Because God is, I am." Relieved by such knowledge, he again turned himself over to God with the simple expression of faith: "Let it happen."

The unspoken private meditations of this contemplative monk also sounded a modern call to action. On one of the first few pages of his prayer book, he quoted Mother Teresa: "You give only what you live." A few pages later, he paraphrased Kant: "If one wills the end, one must will the means." He gave these phrases a chilling contemporary context when, next to one Bible passage exhorting us to have faith in God rather than humans, he wrote "no nukes." He mentioned his concerns about abortion and the 1990–91 American Gulf War against Iraqi dictator Saddam Hussein. He characterized another section of Scripture, one urging us to lay down our lives for others, as a mandate to create a "Civilization of Love." Elsewhere, he observed: "If you know and do not do, you do not know." Finally, in the thin margins adjacent to the Gospel writer Matthew's depiction of the last judgment, Brother Boniface explained that the key to both life and the afterlife is "Love of brother here/now."

Mostly, Brother Boniface's prayer book notes reveal a deep and unmistakable passion for his chosen life as a monk. He sought to model his ministry on that of Jesus, which he saw as "Salvation & Joy NOT judgment and violence." At one place in the missal, he described his vocation: "Our <u>apostolate</u>: hidden, prayer, faithfulness in daily (hour by hour) duties. <u>SILENCE</u>. <u>PRESENCE</u>." One of his many prayer book annotations stands apart and seems to best sum up the man and to capture, in just five words, the essence of his spirit: "Silence, the Pause that refreshes."

When I first met him, the name Boniface seemed formal and long. He signed notes to us with the simple moniker, "Bon," so he became Brother Bon. If you were to cast a man as a monk, he looked the part: bald head, ruddy red checks, and a soft high voice with a slight hint of a Bronx accent. One early monastery photo I saw shows him baking bread and sporting what seems to be a leprechaun-like beard, but no moustache, nicely outlining his ever-shining face.

His gait was particularly striking. He did not walk into a room. He floated in, tall, thin, and gracefully, as if his feet were an inch off the ground, levitated by some unearthly force or hoisted upon his own personal cloud. You could instantly pick him out, based on his movements alone, when he entered the abbey church in the dark. If the church lights were on, you'd notice him already in his assigned seat, motionless, engaged in a deep and intimate conversation with God. However, he would never describe himself in this reverent way. Instead, he preferred something far more modest and unassuming like this self-description: "Look at yourself, Brother. You thought that you were coming to give God glory, and here you find yourself—you're just a stinker."[10]

As we started to visit the monastery regularly, Brother Boniface put us all to work in the bookstore. We stocked, restocked, dusted, cleaned, and helped behind the counter while he interacted with visitors. He was a model of Christian hospitality, or he always thought we were hungry, or maybe both. He regularly appeared with food. This could be simply a Mounds chocolate bar, like the one he once gave my sister Karen on her birthday, wrapped in a small brown paper bag with a handwritten note on it, or it could be a full tray loaded down with a loaf of monk bread, creamed honey, and a pitcher of that strong abbey fresh milk. Accompanying every meal was an impromptu and joyful Brother Bon story about the goodness or love of God.

Soon I became his assistant, or shadow, or maybe just his little buddy. He would see us in the church, and magically appear moments later, often in what looked like a hand-me-down, extremely well-used, heavily patched set of blue coveralls, and a beat-up beanie hat. His style of clothes accurately depicted his style of life. One winter morning we stopped by his room to get something he needed. His sparse living quarters, attached to the side of the bookstore and separate from the main monastic living area, were cold and austere. While he looked for what he needed, I shivered and leaned against his bed waiting, and was amazed that it was like leaning on a rock. I asked him about it. He reached over and pulled away the single wool blanket and cotton sheet that covered the bed to reveal a straw mattress underneath. He was old school; such was the sleeping arrangements for every Trappist in the 1940s, but nearly all of them had taken more comfortable measures in the decades since.

I followed him around the grounds as he went about his workday, doing this or that, managing the bookstore, feeding and caring for the chickens, or maintaining the coops. On days when I was at the monastery early enough, usually right after the monks' regular Mass at 6:20 a.m., Brother Bon often invited me to help with the daily morning ritual of gathering the eggs. At first, I imagined we would be tiptoeing through a straw-filled enclosure, seeking to distract plump, defensive, and skittish hens as we snatched their precious white orbs from underneath them. But my vision of the process was imaginative and cartoonish. The monastery's chicken coop was a sleek model of modern agricultural efficiency and a marvel to behold. It was a huge metal structure, holding 6,000 to 8,000 chickens, all in wire cages, something that would not be wildly popular with animal rights advocates today. At its peak operation, the facility processed more than 6,000 eggs a day. Once the chickens had done their share of the manufacturing work, the eggs would slowly roll along the slightly tilted bottom of the cages and land gently on a conveyor belt below. The belt delicately transported the eggs several hundred feet to a processing room full of various workstations.[11]

At one station, someone cleaned and rinsed them. At another, the eggs on the conveyor would glide over a set of strong lights that illuminated their insides. One of the monks wore special shaded goggles to protect his eyes and monitored the line to detect any bloody, double-yoked or otherwise deficient or rare eggs. These were removed from the conveyor belt. At the next station, eggs were weighed and then, based on weight, sorted by the processing machine into large, medium, or small sizes. They then were redirected to a specific packing station and neatly lined up in two parallel rows, six per row. At that point, a worker would use a special tool with twelve suction cups to gently pick up a dozen eggs at a time and softly place them in a carton. Each carton was marked with the size of the eggs and the Holy Trinity Abbey brand: Mount Ogden Eggs.

These cartons were moved by hand into a box case that contained similar sized eggs, all in one dozen cartons. The cases then were either moved into a large walk-in refrigerator for storage or loaded onto a truck to deliver to those who sold or ordered them, such as the hometown Leon's Market owned by the Sorensen family in nearby Huntsville. Some were saved, of course, for use by the monks in their own cooking or baking. For a time, the monks also sold their eggs to the public in the bookstore.

My job was to help move the cartons into boxes. However, every once in while I was promoted, and got to use the awesome suction-cup device and pack the eggs. Sometimes I was clumsy with the tool and broke an egg, causing bits of shell, yolk, and white to go sailing up into the suction tube, and probably creating a mess that was not fun to clean. Once I got to stay at the station with the bright lights and watch as the eggs were examined for quality. Other times I would try to stay out of the way. I liked to walk around the massive coop and pretend I was talking with the chickens. I never meant to frighten them, but sometimes if I got too close to the cages, wings would flap and feathers would fly.

Brother Bon lovingly tended to his chickens. He would often make indecipherable comforting and reassuring cooing or humming sounds, almost as if he was singing to them. Unlike my own more guttural sounds, the hens recognized his voice and calmed as he walked by. It reminded me of the story I once heard in school about how St. Francis preached to the birds. Our teacher showed us a painting from the upper church of the Basilica of St. Francis in Assisi, created by the Renaissance artist Giotto, which depicts the famous scene. In the painting, more than a dozen birds recline peacefully beneath a tree, watching and listening attentively as Francis tells them how much God loves them and cares for them. Brother Bon did the same thing with his thousands of clucking chickens.

One evening I was walking with Brother Bon in the chicken house when he suddenly stopped to inspect a specific chicken that he did not think was behaving normally. He told me it was sick and that he needed to protect the other chickens. He put on his gloves and delicately removed the bird from the cage and we went outside. For me, Brother Bon was the face of God on earth, and so I rather naively expected he had some sort of wonderful or miraculous cure for the afflicted chicken. He did have a cure, but not the one I expected.

As an expert farmer, he quickly broke the bird's neck and humanely put it out of its fowl misery. I was startled, but I should not have been surprised. He did what any good chicken farmer should have done to protect the rest of the flock. Indeed, because of where they lived, on other occasions the other monks had to similarly deal with other natural threats to their farming operations, such as rodents, gophers, ground squirrels, and even bobcats.[12] When I later told my Mom and sister about the sick chicken's fate, they were surprised, too. Our regard for Brother Bon was so high that we admiringly, but unrealistically, had attributed to him the power to cure sick chickens.

He was practical and resourceful in other ways, too. He started giving us large handfuls of cash, rather amazing for someone who had taken a vow of poverty. The cash was not for us, of course. Rather, for a couple of years, Mom distributed Brother Bon's cash to various charitable causes and regularly added some of her own money to the donation. Even a boy like me could recognize this as his and her versions of the "widow's mite" discussed in the Gospel of Mark: "And he called his disciples to him, and said to them, 'Truly, I say to you, this poor widow has put in more than all those who are contributing to the treasury. For they all contributed out of their abundance; but she out of her poverty has put in everything she had, her whole living.'"[13]

This regular disbursement of the unofficial Boniface Foundation charitable proceeds followed a standard pattern. At Brother Boniface's request, Mom would exchange cash for money orders or bank checks in the amount of the particular donation to be made, and then send them via registered mail to a priest or a nun in India. In turn, the priest and nun used the money for various good works and to help the poor in their communities. I remember two of Brother Bon's beneficiaries well: Father Williams and Sister Gemma.

Father Williams was a young, olive-skinned, handsome, and pleasant priest living in India. Among other things, he used the money to install a clean drinking water system for his poor rural village. He once sent us a photo of him, in his white cassock, standing by part of the facility along with some of his neighbors. We received dozens of chatty thank-you letters from him, reporting in vivid detail about his activities. I'd love to have the chance to read them again today, but we passed all the letters on to Brother Boniface.

Sister Gemma did different, but also important, things with the donations. Her work involved caring for orphans and supporting a school in a different but equally impoverished part of India. She also sent us regular written reports. However, her written English was not as fluent as Father Williams's. Probably reacting to the stark and urgent circumstances where she did her work, she sounded rather blunt and more demanding in her requests for additional funds. Although she kept sending money to Sister Gemma, Mom preferred hearing from Father Williams.

We even sent some of Brother Boniface's money to the Kalaupapa leper colony on the Hawaiian island of Molokai. A Belgian priest, and now a saint, Father Damien de Veuster made the colony famous because he directly cared for the victims of Hansen's disease beginning in 1873. He eventually also contracted, and passed away from, the illness afflicting his patients. His story of compassion and devotion even unto death always fascinated and inspired me. I remember writing once to our contact in Molokai to whom we sent the monastery's donations. I offered to be a pen pal with any of the lepers who might want outside contact. The return letter thanked me for the kind offer, but politely declined, citing the fact that although the disease was controlled, it still was contagious.

I never calculated the total amount of cash involved in these transactions, but Mom must have sent thousands and thousands of dollars, most supplied by Brother Bon, to India and other places with need, during a two or three-year period. Where did a poor monk get all that money? To this day, I am not certain. We used to joke with him that the abbey had special currency-growing trees or its own money-printing machine. My guess is that friends of the monastery gave him charitable contributions and that he simply passed them along to someone else who needed it more than he or the monastery did. Part of the money may have come from his bookstore sales and egg proceeds.

I am certain some of the money came from the monks themselves, who felt it appropriate and necessary to share the bounty of their farm with others in need. Brother Bon confirmed this point in an oral history interview he gave to Weber State University in 1972, saying, "The past few years we have been self-supporting, self-sustaining. And besides that, we have been giving charitable donations around the world, as people have been asking us. In India, Africa, Europe and other parts, even here in America."[14] Wherever it originated, Brother Bon's little informal charitable foundation was a significant force for good as far as 8,000 miles away from his humble room with the straw mattress in Huntsville.

Years later, after all these donations were sent and spent, I learned that Boniface is a revered Catholic name, one carried over the years by prominent popes as well as by the patron saint of Germany. Yet, I think the greatest bearer of that name was our own humble Utah Boniface. His selflessness, generous spirit, and bright demeanor all were reflected in his face. His friend and fellow monk Father Patrick Boyle called him "God's blue-eyed angel." My family put our own personal little spin on his famous name. Because the word "bon" means "good," we just called him Brother Good Face.

I sometimes wish I had recorded the conversations we had. I would like to go back and listen again, perhaps pore over transcripts of the same, and derive new meaning from them. My memories and words here capture only a glimpse of his human spirit and wisdom and kindness, but not the full details of the characteristics of the man. Fortunately, for the sake of a bit more detail, Brother Bon liked to write and distribute notes.

One blogger I have never met recalled a visit he made to the monastery when Brother Boniface floated about and handed out small slips of paper to those attending Mass that day. The papers contained a verse from Micah 6:8 that read, "This is what Yahweh asks of you, only this: to act justly, to love tenderly, and to walk humbly with your God." As he passed out the note, Brother Bon slyly told recipients that, "I like this."[15]

Another friend of the monastery named Flo Earlewine shared online a letter that Brother Boniface had written to her, and which illustrates his writing and speaking style:

> Let Your God Love You. Be Silent. Be Still. Alone. Empty before your God. Say nothing. Ask nothing. Be silent. Be still. Let your God look upon you. That is all. God knows. God understands. God loves you with an enormous love. God only wants to look upon you with love. Quiet. Still. Be. Let your God love you.

I still have two notes he wrote to us, one to Mom, and one to me upon the occasion of my college graduation. He wrote to Mom when she first became an empty nester, when my sister and I had moved away from home. The note is more like a free-form poem than a letter:

> Kay, my sister,
> As children leave home, mother remains.
> In silence, solitude before God, prayers, tears, joys, memories,

petition, love, hope ascend daily heavenward. In fact, also for the many children in our good world who have no one to pray for them.

He signed it, "In Jesus, Bon."

Fittingly, on the front of the college graduation card he sent to me in 1983, there is a painting of a barefoot, brown-robed monk with his arms joyfully outstretched in the direction of a simple wooden cross. The words inside the card, written in his distinctive round handwriting style, are vintage Brother Boniface poetry:

Ave Maria...
Mike, my brother...Congrats.
Discipline, application, commitment always pay off,
we grow as we die.
Hope there was an easier way.
In this Mike you are a good example for modern youth.
Only yesterday you helped me behind the counter, bookstore.
Maybe, in a few years I'll help you behind the "bar." Make mine Canadian Club.
Love Bon.

I think it a profound irony that a penniless monk is one of the richest human beings I will ever know. We never clinked glasses of Canadian Club together, but I sip from his sweet memory nearly every day and raise a grateful toast to the man who saw me when I yearned to be seen, and who picked me for his team.

■ ■ ■

CHAPTER 8

The Slowest Superhero

Being Catholic in my family never was a dip-your-toe-in-it, once-a-week, only-an-hour-on-Sunday, kind of thing. It was more like a deep dive, full immersion, or even obsession, to be undertaken in the most heroic proportions possible.

I consistently attended either Catholic school or catechism classes, then officially called CCD (Confraternity of Christian Doctrine). I sang in the school choir. I served as an altar boy and prayed the Rosary. I walked door-to-door and sold boxes of Catholic Christmas cards as a school fundraiser in the winter. I sold various kinds of (likely illegal) raffle tickets in the fall—tickets for cash prizes always sold best inside and outside the Catholic community. I sold Catholic chocolate candy bars as a school fundraiser in the spring. The skill of selling things to family members, neighbors, and even to total strangers is just one of the many great talents one acquires from a Catholic school education.

I also kept various mementos of the canonized saints. People often wonder why Catholics, in their homes or churches, keep statues or pictures of the saints. Some might even call it idolatry. Catholics do not worship the saints; we look up to them as people who did great things or lived exemplary lives that perhaps we can and should emulate. Remembering them in this tangible way is no different from displaying photos of beloved family members or friends, or admiring great figures of history, much like I keep a bust of Abraham Lincoln in my office.

As a boy I had my own miniature and somewhat tacky shrine, consisting of carefully arranged, plastic statues of the main Catholic sacred action heroes. There was but one significant omission from the shrine: God the Father. In my mind's eye, I always have pictured God the Father as the powerful but benevolent figure from Michelangelo's Sistine Chapel ceiling painting, the gray-bearded older man, with flowing white hair, reaching out his index finger to give life to Adam while supported by representatives of the heavenly host of angels. Yet, I never had, and could never find, a plastic statute of God the Father.

I did have three other critical statues in the shrine. There was Jesus, wearing his red and white robes, with long brown hair and a beard, graphically bearing his sacred heart for all to see. There was Mary, the mother of Jesus, smiling slightly and looking pure and resplendent in her veil and flowing gown of blue and white. She was the closest thing we Catholics had to a feminine presence in the divine hierarchy. I also had a statue of Mary's husband, Joseph the carpenter. Unlike my statues of Jesus and Mary, who both stood on semispherical and blue half globes, my Joseph stood on a plain base, carpenter's hammer in hand. He was the hardworking, down-to-earth, artisan caretaker of the Holy Family. Altogether, it was the classic and conventional nuclear household, and my little shrine honored it, even though my own family no longer resembled it.

The shrine stood on a small nightstand next to my bed. I tended it meticulously. Every so often I would dust and reorganize it and rearrange the statues. I would change the color of the foundational decorative towel or washcloth underneath it (green in March, yellow at Easter, red in December), add new plastic flowers, redesign the Lincoln logs or Legos surrounding the figurines like a decorative fence, or add prayer cards to the setting. Sometimes, at Christmastime, I added a couple of lights, and at Easter, a few fresh blossoms or green leaves from whatever trees or bushes near us were emerging from their winter hibernation. Then, I would proudly call family members into my room for an official public unveiling and rededication.

I also read and cherished my own edition of a picture book called *The New Lives of the Saints*, written by a priest from the Society of the Divine Word. A gift for my First Communion, the book was a series of simple stories, with color illustrations. It was a Catholic version of the modern-day Avengers, or of various other comic book mythic superheroes. The author described the saints as "brothers and sisters in Heaven" who are "worthy of honor, and as friends of God will help you to serve God and save your soul."

The author also kindly explained that the rest of us need not be canonized as saints, but rather could attain this status by "loving God with all your heart, and your neighbor as yourself for the love of God."[1]

Within the pages of *The New Lives of the Saints* some really great stories unfolded. There was the ecologically minded Francis of Assisi, who preached to the birds and tamed a fierce wolf; the intellectual and mystical Teresa of Avila, who levitated; the strong and powerful Christopher, who bore Jesus on his back; the brave and virtuous Joan of Arc, the rare female who led a victorious army; and the quite clever-to-the-end Lawrence the martyr, a man who, as he was being burned alive because of his Christian faith, still had the sense of humor and presence of mind to tell his persecutors to turn him over because he was cooked enough on one side.

My own full name evokes the Irish Catholic superheroes. Michael means "Who is like God?" He is the warrior archangel who battled and defeated Satan and sent him and his legion of fallen angels plummeting into the flames of hell. Patrick is the patron saint of Ireland. He was born in Roman Britannia, and in the middle of the fifth century evangelized the Emerald Isle by famously using the shamrock to explain the mystery of the Holy Trinity. O'Brien means "of Brian," those who descend from Brian Boru, who was the Catholic high king of Ireland beginning in 1002 and who died valiantly fighting Viking invaders at the Battle of Clontarf, near Dublin, in 1014.

Growing up Catholic, with a name like Michael, you hear stories about the meaning and significance of your name. In Catholic art and imagery, Michael is depicted as the powerful winged warrior archangel bearing sword and shield. His epic divine confrontation with Satan is told in the famous story from the book of Revelation, which I regularly heard proclaimed at the monastery, at church, and in school.

The story goes like this:

> And a great portent appeared in heaven, a woman clothed with the sun, with the moon under her feet, and on her head a crown of twelve stars; she was with child and she cried out in her pangs of birth, in anguish for delivery. And another portent appeared in heaven; behold, a great red dragon, with seven heads and ten horns, and seven diadems upon his heads. His tail swept down a third of the stars of heaven, and cast them to the earth. And the dragon stood before the woman who was about to bear a child,

that he might devour her child when she brought it forth; she brought forth a male child, one who is to rule all the nations with a rod of iron, but her child was caught up to God and to his throne, and the woman fled into the wilderness, where she has a place prepared by God, in which to be nourished for one thousand two hundred and sixty days. Now war arose in heaven, Michael and his angels fighting against the dragon; and the dragon and his angels fought, but they were defeated and there was no longer any place for them in heaven. And the great dragon was thrown down, that ancient serpent, who is called the Devil and Satan, the deceiver of the whole world—he was thrown down to the earth, and his angels were thrown down with him.[2]

When I heard this story read at the monastery, I was in the chapel, with the great stained-glass Salve window of Mary looming in the background, just above the shoulders of the reader. With my overactive imagination, I redesigned the window in my mind, adding to it a great red dragon, with seven heads and ten horns, seven diadems on his heads, a tail sweeping away the stars from the sky, and white-winged angels coming to do battle. Sometimes I imagined the great battle playing out as a sort of stained glass video. I loved the window as it was, but I also always thought my redesigned versions would be epic and awesome.

After hearing several Michael stories like this one, I often wondered if I could live up to the reputation of the powerful first name that I bore and wore every day. Eventually, I embraced the fanciful notion that it was the destiny of anyone named Michael to have his own personal war with the great satanic dragon. Unfortunately, certain events occasionally cast serious doubts on my own skills as such a warrior. In my own battles with the forces of Lucifer, I have not always shown the courage of St. Michael. I have not always lived up to the sterling example set by the great archangel of heaven, a topic I have had to raise in the confessional and in requests for forgiveness from others.

Yet, these personal battles did not all turn out so bad. One of the most interesting and memorable played out in my preteen years, about the same time that we started to visit the monastery. The most popular movie playing then was William Peter Blatty's 1973 supernatural thriller, *The Exorcist*. In the film, Linda Blair stars as an innocent girl who is possessed by the devil soon after playing with a Ouija board. The movie depicts the efforts of two priests seeking to exorcise the demons from her. During the exorcism, the possessed child resists them, levitates and spins midair, covers them with regurgitated pea soup, mocks them, and humiliates them. I did not see the movie, but most of my friends did, and I heard a lot of frightening details about it.

Somehow, I got it into my head that Satan was pestering me to purchase my soul. For weeks and months, I turned him down, but he was a persistent little devil. I would reject him but then I kept getting the quiet and whispering sensation in my head that he was asking again. Oddly enough, I do not remember him ever offering anything of value in exchange for such an important prize as my soul. I understood, even in my youthful state, that admitting to having such conversations with the devil might cause others to view me with suspicious eyes. So, I did not tell anyone about my own battles with the great red dragon. But all that changed one night, just after bedtime, when the face-off for my eternal soul felt particularly intense. I decided to tell Mom what was happening.

She had put me to bed, and probably was relieved to have a little quiet time to herself at the end of a long day. I do not remember exactly what she was doing when I paid her my nocturnal visit. I walked up to her and reported, in a matter-of-fact manner, "Mom, the devil is trying to get me to sell my soul to him." She showed great discipline in reacting to my comment. There was no quivering lip, no sign of repressed laughter, but also no reaction to suggest she was thinking that my mind was lost.

She was quiet for a few moments. Finally, she looked at me and said, "Well, don't do it." I said, "OK," and went back to bed. Battle over, I quickly fell asleep.

We never discussed the subject again. She never took me to see a therapist or even an exorcist, although in hindsight I now see she did stop serving split pea soup at dinnertime. She never followed up, even casually, with what would have been logical and appropriate questions: "Honey, did you ever decide whether or not to sell your soul to the devil?" or "Dear, is that nasty Satan fellow still pestering you about your eternal life?" Perhaps she did not follow up because she felt confident I would take her advice, which I did.

I also was blessed, or saddled, with the middle name Patrick, one that, as I've mentioned, has its own esteemed place in the Catholic pantheon of saints and superheroes. St. Patrick is revered not unlike another Patrick I came to know, whom I met at the monastery, a compelling man in his own quiet and unique way. Everyone who visited the monastery, at one time or another, probably met Father Patrick Boyle. He touched many, many lives in a positive way.

At first glance, Father Patrick did not look like a typical superhero. He stood about five feet tall, weighed no more than 125 pounds, and upon meeting him you'd doubt his ability to withstand the winter gales that howled through the abbey property each winter. He had large, protruding ears, a bald head, a kind face, and an infectious smile.[3]

Before he became a monk, his name was John Patrick Boyle. In one of the best instances of self-examination I have known, he decided to dedicate his life to God while still in the sixth grade at a Catholic school in St. Louis, Missouri. As a result, he eventually joined a seminary to study to become a priest. The seminary was his gateway to the monastery. He said, "In the Catholic seminary, I prayed one night and decided if I'm going to do something for God, I'm going all the way. The monastery represented the ultimate dedication for me."[4] He was attracted to Utah's Holy Trinity Abbey in particular "because of its lack of complexity or complications."[5]

He joined the monastery in 1950, after one last trip to the local ballpark to watch his sports hero Stan Musial hit a home run for his beloved St. Louis Cardinals. Stan the Man retired in 1963, but Father Patrick lived at the Utah abbey for almost seventy years, doing so with enthusiasm and vigor, and with his own unique energy. When interviewed in a 2013 documentary film, he said, "Life gets better by the day." He told people that for him, the secret of success has been to just surrender to God and "enjoy the ride."[6] Indeed, the documentary shows him, then at age 85, driving a riding mower across the abbey lawn with a big grin across his face.[7] He always was ready for the next adventure, telling people, "Well, I'll see you in Heaven! I've got my bags packed!"[8]

People instantly loved him, in part because he had a calm demeanor and self-deprecating sense of humor. Whenever he was asked about the abbey's wheat bread, which was often, he smiled and quipped that it was more popular than the monks. When asked why the monastery had stopped making honey, he would note that they did not run out of bees, they ran out of monks. He would tell bookstore customers they could take home anything there except a monk. And his favorite joke was to ask, "Do you know the difference between a monk and a monkey? A monkey has a tail!"

Although he started almost every conversation with a similar joke, he would quickly and smoothly transition to a discussion about his favorite topic, God's love. He would often say: "When you walked through that door, Christ came into this room!" And he liked to remind people that the past is past, that God is in charge of the future, and thus we all should live in the present moment.

As a result of this belief, he was certain and deliberate, and to some eyes, slow in his actions and movements, including his walk and gestures. Why? He lived in and relished the moment. For example, there is a point in the Catholic Mass where the celebrating priest consecrates the bread and wine on the altar into the body and blood of Christ. Catholics use the lofty theological word "transubstantiation" to describe this consequential moment. As the consecration occurs, the priest, in sequence, holds up first the bread/body and then the wine/blood for all to see. Priests have a variety of styles for doing this display. Some adopt the most efficient approach, a sort of run-and-gun, look-quickly-or–you-will-miss-it, rapid-up-and-rapid-down technique. One priest I knew could say the entire Mass in about six or seven minutes, and with him, if you blinked at the wrong time, you would miss the entire transubstantiation moment. Other priests would hold the bread and cup up for longer and move it carefully along the line of the horizon for all to see. Father Patrick was in a league of his own at this part of the Mass. He would reverently and devotedly hold up the bread/body and linger, and linger, and linger, sometimes for what felt like eternity. It probably was just for a minute or two (OK, maybe three or four or five minutes) if you counted the time. Father Patrick's consecration concentration and Eucharistic stamina constantly impressed me.

One time, just as Father Patrick raised the cup into the air, my nose started running. Despite my being raised at a monastery, my nasal crisis was more important at that moment than the Mass unfolding before me. I leaned back (we always knelt during the consecration) and looked through my pants pockets for a tissue. I did not have one, so I checked my coat pocket, but there was nothing there either. I leaned over to my sister and asked if she had a tissue. She looked, and mouthed the word "no." Perturbed and snotty, I asked her, "Why not?" She did not respond. Instead, although she always has been a far better person than me, she gave me a sort of piercing look that only a sister can give to a brother. Mom noticed all the activity going on behind her, so she turned around, gave us her own look, and shushed us both. Left with no other options, I wiped my nose on my sleeve and kneeled again. Meanwhile, Father Patrick was calmly holding up the chalice and still in the middle of the consecration.

I also was amazed at how Father Patrick would gaze at what he was holding during the consecration, the bread or the wine, the body and blood of Christ, almost as if he had forgotten about the rest of us in the church. Caught up in the moment, he seemed to be staring adoringly into the eyes of someone or something that he loved deeply. Of course, this is exactly what he was doing. It took a long time to get through his Mass, but when he was done, you really felt like you had been to Mass.

The same was true with his blessings. Catholic priests give blessings for all sorts of things (rosaries, medals, other religious items) and for every imaginable occasion. There are blessings for the sick, blessings for those going on a long journey, blessings to protect your throat from sickness and disease, blessings for pets, blessings for those with troubled hearts seeking peace, blessings to help you win sporting events, and also ordinary, everyday blessings to help you on your way. Father Patrick would freely give a blessing to anyone who wanted one, and sometimes would offer a blessing even if you did not ask for one. My guess is that he blessed hundreds of thousands, Catholics and non-Catholics alike, an impressive legacy for any minister of God. He also adapted to the changing times and technologies. Once he blessed me by way of a telephone voice message machine.

As he gave his blessing, he would say, "May the blessing of Almighty God, the Father, Son and Holy Spirit, descend upon you and remain with you always." As he spoke, he would briefly and gently touch the top of your head in an apostolic fashion. The effect was almost electrical. You could feel the blessing coursing and tingling through your body, from the top of your head to the tips of your toes. As with his celebration of the Mass, it took longer than average to complete this special blessing, but again, when Father Patrick blessed you, you knew you had been blessed.

He told others that being alone is not being aloof, that in the quiet of his monastic solitude he still knew of the wars and disasters of the world, and "those rumblings reverberate more deeply within the heart." Despite his close to seven decades of living a chosen life of solitude, he said, "People mean a great deal to me. Everyone who visits is of great value to me." His years at Holy Trinity Abbey taught him that the challenge of modern life was keeping faith that God will continue to reveal himself. In 2000, as one millennium passed into another, he said, "Years ago I learned about the workability of hope. Every day I try to cultivate the virtue of hope. I've cultivated it for [over] fifty years now. And you know something? It works."[9]

During his time at the monastery, I think Father Patrick evolved into God's version of a priestly turtle. This was his superpower. He never had to run quickly around the bases of life because, like his St. Louis Cardinals hero Stan Musial, he hit a vocational home run. He took his time to get where he was going, and he enjoyed where he was at any given moment along the way, but always reached his destination, growing and going slowly, gently, kindly, honorably, but with great power. Because of this sweet tortoise-like mental image I developed of him, I was surprised when he and Mom one day began debating which of them could move faster. She was confident in her abilities and conditioning, given that her job kept her on her feet moving quickly around a restaurant for up to ten hours a day. He good-naturedly challenged her to a race down the Abbey Road, and Mom accepted.

The big race never occurred, but it was amusing to hear Mom and one of her beloved monks have a little trash talk about it from time to time. I do not know who would have won. I always was certain, however, that if the road to heaven was a race, my own Catholic superhero, Father Patrick, would get there ahead of me, slowly and surely, but then stop, turn around, and cheer me on as I slowly struggled in my own divine marathon.

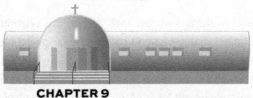

CHAPTER 9

Chasing Cows

ONE OF THE HALLMARKS OF THE MONASTIC MOVEMENT IS ITS emphasis on blending *ora et labora,* which is Latin for prayer and work. I was (and still am) a work in progress on both fronts. I was not a lazy boy. I was responsible and dependable and did well in school. Yet, I could not claim the title of hardest working teenager of my day, especially as my friends the monks defined work.

For a time, I delivered *TV Guide* magazines and then the *Ogden Standard-Examiner* to our neighbors. One harsh critic of the newspaper once told me I was working for the "Sub-Standard Exaggerator," but I thought it was a pretty good paper. I also flipped burgers, poured milkshakes, and fried potatoes at McDonalds for one summer, and served up spicy Mexican American food at a takeout joint called Taco Johns during another. Right after high school and before college, I worked as a cub reporter at the *Ogden Standard-Examiner.* I also worked various odd jobs.

My *labora* ethic also was limited because I did not grow up in a traditional boy world. No one taught me how to use hand tools, or operate landscaping equipment, or to fix a car, and so I never really developed any such skills or interests. (My poor son Daniel Patrick may suffer the same fate.) My family jokes that there are two kinds of people in the world, those who fix things and those who break them. They always firmly, but affectionately, put me in the second of these categories.

Although I lacked industrial skills, I recognized industriousness when I saw it, and I saw it at the monastery. Often it was at work with the monks that I came to know and learn from them best. Manual work was an integral part of their life. St. Benedict's Rule states, "When they live by the labor of their hands, as our fathers and the apostles did, then they are really monks."[1] They also had to work hard for more practical reasons. They had a large operation and a lot of mouths to feed. Thomas Merton described what his busy brothers did each workday at Gethsemani in 1946, including cooking, cleaning, fixing, painting, sweeping, mopping, collecting honey, typing, driving tractors, fighting with stubborn mules, and worrying about rabbits. He also noted that one monk was making plans for the new Utah monastery.[2]

The scope of work was not much different in Utah by the time I was watching the monks and learning from them. One of the most important jobs was the position of doorkeeper or porter. This was the monk who locked up the church each night after the prayer service of Compline. The Rule of St. Benedict provides, "A wise old monk should guard the gates of the monastery. He should know how to receive and answer a question, and be old enough so he will not be able to wander far."[3] Different monks did this job over the years, and we often exchanged greetings with them after we attended the final monastery chant of the night.

Brother Felix held the keys for a time, and he was always ready to share a corny joke with a nugget of wisdom. Early each July, he would say, "If you go with a fifth on the fourth, then you won't be able to go forth on the fifth!" He also loved to sing a verse or two, usually an Irish ditty. With tongue in cheek, his friend Brother Nicholas Prinster often said Brother Felix "thought he had a good voice." Like Mom, Brother Felix lost his mother at a young age, and his father was an alcoholic.[4] He once gave us a photo of himself, and on the back of the photo, Mom fondly wrote, "His Lordship himself, first to guide me to the monastery, my Brother Felix."

We also met several other porters. One was a friendly newcomer, Father Leander Dosch. He had transferred to Utah from another monastery. Another doorkeeper, the aptly named Father Thomas Porter, had an infectious laugh and a serene nature. Like most of the monks, however, he was more than appeared on the surface, as he also had served for a time as a Trappist scholar (censor) assigned to read and approve Merton's writings.

Brother Edward Eick, who also sometimes worked as guest master, would softly hum and bounce on his feet when he talked with you. He served in the U.S. Army during World War II. He encouraged me to write, giving me my first typewriter, a manual Smith Corona Pacemaker, with old-fashioned ink ribbon and all, that probably dated to the late 1950s or early 1960s. In eighth grade, at age thirteen, I used that typewriter to compose my first published piece, a Letter to the Editor of the *Ogden Standard-Examiner*.

We had many wonderful chats with Brother (soon to be Father) David Altman while he was locking the doors. He joined the monastery in 1966 after reading Merton's autobiography. He was studying to become a priest, so he would give us regular updates on his progress. He told us about his pre-monk life, serving in the Army, attending Temple University in Philadelphia, growing up Jewish, and about how his family did not always understand his vocation. He talked about traveling and working as an accountant, and also about dating California girls. He had a clever and exuberant sense of humor, once trying to help us with an umbrella and accidentally turning it inside out instead. We have a great photo of him smiling and pretending to shield himself from the rain with the defective umbrella. He told a news reporter that he had made the transition from outside life to monastic life the same way that a flea eats an elephant—"one bite at a time."[5]

In the 1970s, the total abbey property included 1,800 acres. The monks used more than half of this as rangeland to support a herd of cattle. They grew crops on about 700 of their cultivated acres, including wheat, alfalfa, barley, and hay. For many years, they irrigated their lands by using large pipes that they moved by hand. I remember seeing both the older and younger brothers in the fields carrying the heavy pipes. They wore blue farmer overalls and safari pith helmets to shield themselves from the sun. It looked like strenuous work.

The farm included the dairy herd I visited on my first tour; it had to be milked twice a day. An older boy I knew, in high school, often came to the monastery to help Father Joseph with milking duties. He was troubled, but working with Father Joseph seemed to help him. The monks had to gather eggs each morning from several thousand chickens. There also were several mechanical shops that the monks used to maintain their equipment. They had tractors and trucks and various other agricultural implements. They even had their own gas pump. The mountain valley setting for this outdoor work matched well with the philosophy of the Trappist life: "Our monasteries are normally located in the countryside, surrounded by natural quiet and beauty, keeping us close to the earth of which God has made us stewards."[6]

There also was a lot of hard work for the monks to do indoors. They maintained their honey, bread, and egg businesses. Several monks worked on the business side of the farm, managing accounts, paying bills, balancing the books, and administering day-to-day affairs. Because the monks lived where they worked, the daily jobs also included tending to their large home. They cleaned the church and other buildings, tended to the grounds and their small cemetery, operated the bookstore, did the laundry, sewed and mended their clothes, cooked meals for each other and guests, washed the dishes, painted, fixed fixtures when they broke, cared for their sick, mowed the lawns, and planted flowers, trees, and gardens. They also did scholarly work, such as reading, studying, writing, editing journals, or organizing classes for each other on various spiritual topics.

As I got to know the monks, and as they became more familiar with me, they began inviting me "behind the scenes" to help, or perhaps more accurately, to allow me to pretend to help them do their work. Most frequently, I helped in the bookstore. I started by cleaning and dusting items and stocking shelves. I remember that as I worked, I noticed on the books the many exotic last names of Catholic authors, such as Teilhard de Chardin, Küng, Congar, and Schillebeeckx. As I proved myself able to handle more responsibility, I was "promoted" to work behind the counter, attend to customers, fill specific orders, and sometimes even act as cashier. It must have been unexpected and comical to some bookstore visitors to see such a youthful face behind the counter, and once one of these customers joked how I must be one of the veteran monks.

My primary supervisors were Brother Felix, Father Patrick, and Brother Boniface. I think in many ways they tolerated me, as I doubt that I dramatically enhanced the efficiency of the operation. On the other hand, they did not seem to mind the help or the company, as it freed them up to do things I think they preferred to do anyway, such as mingle among, interact with, and minister to the abbey's visitors.

Brother Isidore made sure my monastic working experiences were not limited to sales and customer service. He asked me to join him on the farm several times, and despite my being a city boy, I enjoyed these excursions. He took me to plow one of the fields. The monastery's fields were unique: the monks named each one after a saint. Brother Isidore and I plowed the field named for St. Bernard. Other fields were named for St. John the Baptist, St. James, St. Stephen, St. Lucy, St. Benedict, St. Pius, and many others. Brother Isidore would climb up on a huge tractor and pull me up beside him. I had never been on a tractor before. It moved steadily, but it also seemed, at least to my urban senses, to shake tremendously. Occasionally, I steered the tractor and drove it by myself. I felt powerful. I am confident my plowing efforts led to a bumper crop of something in at least one of the sainted fields during that particular growing season.

One time when we were at the monastery for Sunday Mass, I was dressed in nice clothes and shoes, but Brother Izzy appeared and announced that he needed my help afterwards. He and I and some other monks drove to one of the grazing fields, where a lone and rebellious calf was loose. My job was to redirect the calf to the right field.

The monks instructed me to walk the approximate fifty yards to where the defiant calf stood. It had recently rained. I sloshed through the mud, church shoes and all, to confront my adversary. He was shorter and stouter than me, but had an extra set of legs, which I should have recognized gave him a distinct advantage in a footrace. The calf arrogantly glanced up at me. The reproachful, mocking look on its face proclaimed, *Bring it on, rookie!*

In my encyclopedias, I had read that it is a wise military strategy to try to outflank an opponent. Accordingly, I circled around in a flanking maneuver and walked up to the calf, arms wide to both sides to make myself seem larger and more imposing, but also to try to gently direct it back toward the field where the monks wanted it to graze. The calf ignored me until I got within about three or four feet, when it suddenly snorted, bolted sharply to the left, and moved faster than I had ever imagined a calf could move. Within seconds, the calf was about twenty feet behind me again, peacefully grazing as if nothing had happened.

I circled around again, walked up to it, and once more directed it, this time more forcefully and more loudly, but with the same result. This emerging pattern repeated itself several times. After about fifteen minutes or so of this pathetic excuse for herding, the calf was about fifty to a hundred yards farther away from the place where the monks wanted it to be than when we started. I began to wish I had more closely watched the calf ropers at the rodeo. Alas, I had no roping skills, and, more critically, no rope. I am not even sure what I would have done with the crazy calf had I been able to rope it. The calf outweighed me, had home-field advantage, and if roped likely would have dragged me around the pasture at will.

After another quarter hour had passed, the calf grew weary of dealing with such an unskilled but determined amateur cowboy. It finally snorted and moved off in the necessary direction, making it quite clear it was doing so by choice and not due to any of my efforts. The calf haughtily trotted over and joined its mates. Exhausted and muddy, I triumphantly walked back with a John Wayne swagger in my step and rejoined the monks. They were leaning up against their truck watching the whole scene unfold. They complimented me kindly.

As the years have passed, I often have reflected on my encounter in the muddy field with that stubborn monastery calf. Surely, these monks, these grown men, these veteran farmers and ranchers, knew how to handle a runaway calf without my help. So why involve me? Maybe it was an initiation into Future Monks of America. Perhaps they intended it as an opportunity to help a city slicker get his country legs. With the enhanced sensory perception that hindsight provides, however, another possible and more likely motive has emerged. Even now, I can almost hear echoes of the monks quietly and good-naturedly laughing at the situation. In a diversion from their daily mystical encounters with the divine, they might have been engaged in a bit of earthly mischief and pranking that day.

Yes, it must have been one of the oldest tricks in some ancient monastic book: a Trappist version of a snipe hunt. I have reread the Rule of St. Benedict, searching for a chapter or section sanctioning this particular monk activity. I am still looking.

■ ■ ■

CHAPTER 10

The Seasons of Abbey Life

D URING THE SUMMER, THE MONASTERY WAS BEEHIVE GOLDEN, humming and bustling with activity, reminding me now of how Thomas Merton used to complain that Trappist monasteries "produce very few pure contemplatives" because of the busy life.[1] The days grew calmer in autumn, after the harvest, when the green leaves transformed into hues of orange, yellow, red, and brown. In winter, the abbey settled into a cold serenity, a peaceful and silvery solitude. In the busy spring, trees and crops greened, and flowers bloomed pink, white, and yellow; it was the season of resurrection and paschal alleluias.

A monastery abides through circadian rhythms, turns of seasons, and cycles of life. Visitors arrive and depart. Candidates for the monastic life come and go; some become brothers and members of the community and some do not. Brothers become priests. Priests and brothers alike grow old, get sick, and die. I saw many intimate moments of monastic formation and transformation during my decade visiting the monastery, giving special meaning to the biblical admonition that "to everything there is a season and a time for every matter under heaven."[2]

"Admission to the religious life should not be made easy for newcomers," states the Rule of St. Benedict. "As the Apostle says, 'try the spirits if they be of God.'"[3] Accordingly, a man interested in joining the Order of Cistercians of the Strict Observance follows a defined, challenging, and well-trod path.[4] He starts as a candidate/observer, and in this role spends time discussing his possible vocation with other monks and living with the monks for a short period of time to understand and experience what their life is really like. This is an emerging relationship marked by both hope and uncertainty.

After living with the monks and wearing street clothes for a period of time, the observer then must leave the monastery and return to his regular secular life for several weeks or months. If there is mutual interest thereafter, the candidate can rejoin the community as a postulant (meaning someone who applies or asks for something). He then dons a simple white robe as his habit and begins the official formation process. After several months of instruction, the postulant becomes a novice, continues to wear white robes, and after two more years may be invited to take temporary vows. "The years of temporary profession are a time for further study and absorption of the monastic way of living the Gospel, and deeper integration into the community."[5] After at least three, but not more than nine years of living under temporary vows, the monk in training may be allowed to take final vows for life. On this important question, regarding who can join their ranks, the monastery was a pure democracy. The monks voted on every candidate.

We knew several young men who participated in some part of this formation process. Of course, Brothers Jonathan and Gregory were the first ones we met, and the first ones to whom we said goodbye. Another young man, formerly a member of a professional ballet company, was part of the community for a few years. No doubt from years of performance and training, he had a distinctly graceful manner of entering the chapel for services. His name was Brother Joseph Rosario. I liked that name and privately called him "Rosary Joe." He did not stay either. A number of others also arrived and departed.

There was, during our time, one young man we knew who came and stayed the whole time. This was Brother Lawrence (David) Baumbach from Riverside, California. He arrived at Holy Trinity in 1973, fresh off a stint in the Air Force. I remember him as fast talking, bespectacled, and kind. We liked him immediately. In a news interview, he explained, "I visited this monastery on retreat during College years. I liked it. My mother grew up in Utah, so it was a natural to come to Holy Trinity Abbey."[6] We watched him study and work hard for six years and progress through each of the monastic formation stages until he eventually was invited to take final vows. In the summer of 1979, he invited us to attend his solemn profession, the only time I was privileged to watch such an important part of monastic life.

The ceremony for a Trappist's final profession of vows is simple but elegant and full of joy. In many ways, it is like a wedding. Detailed planning occurred, and Brother Lawrence's parents and family attended and helped him celebrate. Brother Lawrence's ceremony started at 6:30 in the morning, with a warm welcome from the abbot, Father Manny, and an exhortation of what it means to live the monastic life. After an opening prayer and hymn, Brother Lawrence professed his five solemn vows. He made promises the monks describe as: "celibacy, of poverty, of obedience in all things good, of stability (meaning that he remains a member of this community), [and] conversion of manners (that is, to live the monastic life to its fullest, without ever saying to himself that he has done enough)."[7]

At one point in the ceremony, Brother Lawrence lay prostrate on the ground in front of the altar, in the reflected light of the Salve window. This was a gesture of his devotion and humility, and also symbolic of the type of pose he eventually would assume again when the time came for the end of his life as a monk. At this moment, face down on the floor, perhaps Brother Lawrence experienced the same thoughts and emotions as did Merton when he made similar vows at Gethsemani Abbey three decades earlier: "I began to laugh, and with my mouth in the dust, because without knowing how or why, I had actually done the right thing, and even an astounding thing."[8]

After the profession of vows, the new monk was blessed and consecrated, and he received the monastic scapular, the black overlay of the Trappist habit. Then, each of his new brothers individually embraced him warmly to formally welcome him to the community. A nice reception followed. The moving ceremony was similar to the only other monastic formation ceremony we witnessed at Holy Trinity Abbey, which was the ordination of Brother David Altman as a priest.

This ordination Mass, in the fall of 1979, followed an ancient Catholic rite, and Utah's Bishop Joseph Lennox Federal presided. He laid his hands on Brother David, vested him in priestly robes (stole and chasuble), gave him a chalice, and anointed his hands with sacred oils. The bishop said a prayer of consecration. Afterward, Brother David lay prostrate on the ground, again showing his humility and, like Brother Lawrence before him, foreshadowing the same position he would occupy at the end of his life as a monk. Now to be called Father David, he then joyfully received the enthusiastic greetings, hugs, and blessings of his fellow Trappists.

Just as I witnessed moments of new life, in the professions of final vows and ordinations, I also saw end-of-life moments. One summer, we met Brother Ferdinand Pfeil, who, at age 79, was the oldest living member of the community at that time. A tailor and bread maker, he was one of the original monks to travel from Gethsemani to establish the abbey. The youngster in me initially was intrigued with him, but for a silly reason. I had not previously heard of anyone named Ferdinand who was not a peace-loving bull preoccupied with sitting alone in a field and smelling flowers.

We did not spend a great deal of time with or really get to know Brother Ferdinand well, but he was beloved by his brothers. He was thin, grandfatherly, wore glasses, and spoke with a slight German accent. Brothers Jonathan and Gregory told us that in English, the word "Pfeil" means bolt or dart, and that his pre-monastery name was William. Thus, the brothers affectionately called Brother Ferdinand "Willie Arrow," one of the best nicknames I have heard.

Brother Ferdinand had a reputation for sweet and childlike rebellion and playfulness, almost like a monastic version of Tom Sawyer or, again, Ferdinand the Bull. He frequently talked while sewing, despite the Trappist rules of silence. More amusingly, he would sneak off to what he thought was an isolated and undiscovered part of the property. One day, another monk stumbled across him there and found that Brother Ferdinand had built an earthen track amid reeds growing alongside the banks of an irrigation canal. Naked, and covered with mud, he was using it for a slide, laughing as he made splash landings in the water. The spying monk reported Brother Ferdinand to the abbot for being "seriously immodest."[9]

We have one photo of Brother Ferdinand walking outside the abbey church, fully clothed and free of mud, on a warm summer day in 1972. A bright light shines like an aura in the lower right-hand corner of the picture, perhaps a processing defect or just bad photography. Mom, however, called such images "Holy Spirit" photos, meaning, in more modern terms, that the light of the Holy Spirit had photobombed the shot. Interestingly, we have similar Spirit-bombed photos of some of the other monks, too. Maybe Mom was on to something.

Brother Ferdinand died about a year later, in 1973, and the monks invited us to attend our first Trappist burial service. Brother Ferdinand's funeral was unlike any I had attended as an altar boy. For a Trappist, death is not a sad event, but the fulfillment of a lifelong yearning for a deeper relationship with God. Merton described it well when he recalled seeing one of the deceased monks from Gethsemani "with that grim smile of satisfaction that Trappist corpses have."[10] Trappists are not morbid and do not actively seek out death. When it arrives, however, they do not fear it as an enemy, but instead welcome it as a beloved brother.

Monks even have a slightly dark sense of humor about the subject. When Holy Trinity Abbey was first established, a newspaper reporter wrote that no one had died yet at the monastery, but that the abbot had "humorously" invited someone to do so. A monk there explained, "You see, we don't think we really have our roots in a place until someone is buried there." The same monk also noted, "We had a fellow in the dispensary a little while ago who we thought might take Father Abbot up on it—but he changed his mind."[11]

In a touching and traditional rite the night before Brother Ferdinand's Resurrection Mass, the members of his monastic fraternity took turns holding vigil over his body, which was laid out in the church on a wooden bier, neither preserved nor embalmed in any way, and clad in his simple white monastic robes. Each brother spent time in contemplation at Brother Ferdinand's feet, taking time to pray for the repose of his immortal soul and to say a few personal words of farewell to a family member.

Early the next morning, the monks celebrated the traditional funeral Mass and engaged in one last set of Gregorian chants in the physical presence of the departed. While serving at funerals during my altar boy days, I learned to love the comforting poetry of the Twenty-third Psalm, which the monks prayed for Brother Ferdinand:

The LORD is my shepherd, I shall not want; he makes me lie down
in green pastures.
He leads me beside still waters; he restores my soul.
He leads me in paths of righteousness for his name's sake.

Even though I walk through the valley of the shadow of death,
I fear no evil;
for thou art with me, thy rod and thy staff, they comfort me.
Thou preparest a table before me in the presence of my enemies;
thou anointest my head with oil, my cup overflows.
Surely goodness and mercy shall follow me all the days of my life;
and I shall dwell in the house of the LORD forever.

At the end of the Mass, the abbey bells slowly tolled, and his brothers carried Brother Ferdinand to the small cemetery adjoining the church, once described this way:

And as final resting places go, this is as scenic as they come. A stately spruce throws shade across one corner of the graveyard, where some brothers doze in lawn chairs in the afternoon. Snowcapped mountains rise to the west. A field of aromatic alfalfa grows to within a few feet of the plots. Bells chime. A robin spends much of its day perched atop the grave markers, warbling now and then.[12]

At the quaint cemetery, a deep rectangular hole waited for Brother Ferdinand. It was just a hole. There was no coffin and no vault. At the graveside, Father Manny proclaimed the familiar, poetic, and beautiful burial benediction:

Eternal rest grant unto his soul, oh Lord,
and may the perpetual light shine upon him.
May his soul, and the souls of all the faithful departed,
through the mercy of God, rest in peace. Amen.

Whenever I hear this benediction, that a perpetual light will shine on a loved one, I feel remarkably consoled and comforted.

Brother Ferdinand's face was covered with a white cloth (perhaps his napkin from the refectory) and several of his brothers, using straps, lowered his body into the grave. Father Brendan was waiting down there, wearing his blue coveralls. As director of the infirmary, he had cared for Brother Ferdinand before death came calling. He tended to him once more now as he gently received his brother's body and guided it to a final resting place. He climbed out of the hole on a small ladder and, along with several other monks, picked up shovels and completely covered the body with a layer of dirt as the service ended. Later, the monks filled in the grave completely, and placed a small white cross, bearing only Brother Ferdinand's name and his dates of birth and death, atop the site.

That was all that there was to it. Merton contrasted this kind of stark "immensely clean" burial to those he had seen in the secular world before he became a monk, which he called a "nightmare of fake luxury and flowers with which the world tries to disguise the fact of death." Merton said the burial of a monk is not frightening, and rather "it is those embalmed corpses rouged up to look like wax-works and couched in satin cushions that terrify the heart and make the healthy smell of flowers horrible by the association."[13] Later explaining the minimalist nature of the Trappist burial service, Father Leander Dosch, who also served as a Utah abbot, said, "We brought nothing into this world, and it's certain we can carry nothing out."[14]

This Trappist introduction to mortality steeled me to face and understand more direct brushes with death. On a cold, overcast Ogden morning in 1974, I left our apartment for a short, but typically uneventful, walk to my grade school a few blocks away. Depending on the day and wind direction, our west side neighborhood smelled like either death or life. A nearby animal byproducts rendering plant often unleashed a pungent, rotten odor that seemed to seep into your flesh and corrupt it. Yet, on many other days, I floated to school carried upon the lilting scent of freshly baked rolls and pastries, courtesy of the local Wonder Bread Hostess factory.

On one such aromatic bread day, a screech of wheels, a thud, a whimper, and the sound of a car speeding away jolted me out of my bakery-induced bliss. I looked across the street and saw the victim of a hit and run, a small dog lying in the gutter. I rushed over to the site of the action, just in time to be the last living thing the dying animal saw. The dog shuddered and grew progressively stiff as a visible wave of rigor mortis swept relentlessly over it, from tail to snout.

I was stunned and sad and . . . fascinated. Never having witnessed it, I had guessed death would be grander, a momentous occasion, but it arrived unceremoniously, without heralding trumpets, in a stealthy and businesslike manner. Then it was gone again, like any other fleeting moment. Right afterwards, a woman, apparently the dog's owner, rushed out of her ground level tenement and looked over the scene. Our mouths never moved. Our eyes spoke to each other. She went back inside and got an old blanket. I helped her wrap up the dead dog and carry it back to her doorstep. She nodded. I left and went on to school. The smell of bread had dissipated, replaced by the fumes from the rendering plant.

I was several minutes tardy, and in the doorway encountered the looming figure of our principal, Mr. Frank Roe. He asked why I was late, and I told him the story. He frowned, scribbled something on a pad of paper, and handed me a note to give my teacher. The note said, "Excused — act of kindness." Mr. Roe was an unusual fellow. He was a large man who wore tiny black glasses perched ever so precariously on the tip of his nose. He called us "pupils," gestured wildly when he taught, and pointed using his middle (instead of his index) finger. This particular eccentricity made us snicker as he flipped off the chalkboard and then the entire class whenever he turned around. Once, while a friend and I helped him move some boxes, he told us about his dream to start his own science academy, which would meet outdoors even in the winter. I asked him about the snow and cold. He responded, "Our science classes will control the weather!" My friend looked at me and rolled his eyes.

Mr. Roe held the job of principal for only two or three years. I do not know why he left. At about the same time his wife, our music teacher, was quite sick with breast cancer. I never spoke with either of them again. Years later, I heard that Mr. Roe had lovingly and tenderly cared for his wife until she succumbed to the cancer. Immediately, I regretted how we had mocked Mr. Roe's quirkiness and strange mannerisms. Knowing what I now know about life, I suspect some of Mr. Roe's odd ways were due to the stressful onset of Mrs. Roe's illness. Upon hearing the news about how he had nursed his sick wife, I longed to tell Mr. Roe that his strangeness was okay, that some quirky out-of-the-norm behavior is understandable, and maybe even expected, when you are facing death. I wanted to hand him the same note he gave me, one that said: "Excused — act of kindness."

Brother Ferdinand's death was not only a new beginning for him, but also a portal of sorts for us at the monastery. After we attended his funeral Mass, many of the other monks we had not known well also began to regard us as part of the family. One of them who had seemed distant at first now started to acknowledge my mother's regular presence at the 6:30 a.m. Mass by changing his standard verbal greeting of "my dear brothers" to a more inclusive "my dear brothers and sister." Eventually, we became friends with that monk, Father Denis Murphy. He looked like a cookie jar version of a monk—short, stout, and stern. If monks were Disney dwarves, we would have called him Grumpy, based on his serious demeanor and apparent scowl when he entered the church. Appearances, however, are deceiving.

Rather than stern or grumpy, Father Denis was a soulful, gregarious, and affable Irish teddy bear. We had mistaken his stern face as he entered the church for what really was a face deeply focused on prayer and contemplation. He was born in 1896 and served in the military during World War I. A friend told me Fr. Denis had worked as an office boy for the great inventor Thomas Edison. He had been a monk at Gethsemani and helped found Holy Trinity Abbey in 1947. He succeeded Brother Ferdinand as the oldest living Trappist in Huntsville. In a short time, I came to love him dearly and tried to visit him whenever I could.

He was a bookkeeper and, as treasurer, handled the monastery's money. When I visited him in the business office, he would joke about how he had set some money aside for himself in a Swiss bank account. One day, when Mom went to the early morning Mass, he surprised her afterward with a breakfast tray of wheat toast and coffee. They ate it together in the back of the church. In a sign of familial comfort, he pulled out his false teeth in front of her while he ate. This is just my speculation, but I think if we had stopped visiting the abbey after the summer of the folk Masses, the monks would have thought of us as just passing by. Because we paid more regular visits over time, I guess we developed a certain insider status that made it possible to meet wonderful folks like Father Denis.

Monks are supposed to be happy for each other when they die, but I was sad and upset when Father Denis passed away in early August 1982. Other than Brother Ferdinand's burial, his was the only other Trappist funeral I attended. As I followed the procession on our way to the cemetery, I saw one of the novices I knew somberly tolling the bells in honor of Father Denis. He looked sad. I was overwhelmed by the emotion of that moment. By now I was a young man in college. Intellectually, I understood that Father Denis's soul had graduated, as the monks liked to say, to heaven, and was in a better place, and that this was the culmination of his life's vocation. Nevertheless, perhaps more selfishly, I missed my friend. I wept for him.

■ ■ ■

CHAPTER 11

Monastic Winter

T HE MONASTERY WAS SYMBIOTICALLY MARRIED TO THE NATURAL WORLD that surrounded it. This was especially true in winter.

Huntsville is in a mountain valley. Cold weather temperatures can be harsh and winter conditions unforgiving. A 1951 newspaper report noted that on one frigid day, temperatures plunged to forty degrees below zero at Holy Trinity Abbey. The Ogden Valley's average annual snowfall is over six feet. From December to February, the average low temperature in Huntsville, with its elevation at just under 5,000 feet, is a mere nine degrees above zero. The average high is barely above the freezing mark. I even remember some cold summer monastery mornings in Huntsville.[1]

I do not like to be cold. Given this thermal inclination, for two or three months of the year, my personal search for truth and meaning at the monastery coincided with, and at times was replaced by, an urgent search for heating vents. This was not exactly a new quest for me. At home, during the winter months, I often wrapped up and sat on heating vents, using a blanket to capture the heat and create a bubble of warm air. On cold school-day mornings, I locked myself in the bathroom and fell back asleep on the vent. This irritated Mom to no end, because she was trying to get me to school on time. She pounded on the door, reminded me of the time, and demanded to know if I had gone back to sleep. With a weak and drowsy voice, I denied dozing off and then finally started getting ready for school. She predicted that my own kids would do the same thing to me some day and then I would know how she felt. They did. I do.

One of the monks told me the story of how difficult it was during their first two winters in the Ogden Valley. Not only was it cold, but also they were living in thin-walled, surplus wooden military barracks with a barely functioning temporary heating system. In the face of these challenges, one clever monk volunteered to tend to the chickens during this time. Going above and beyond the call of duty, he quite willingly spent extra hours on the job in the well-heated coop hatchery with his fine-feathered friends and their eggs.

My own search for Holy Trinity heat ended not in the chicken coop, but in the elegantly simple monastery church. The beautiful church was large, stark, and quite cold. One frigid winter's night we arrived there early, for Compline, which would not start for another thirty minutes. The church was completely dark and overwhelmingly peaceful and quiet. Mom and Karen went upstairs. I decided to stay downstairs and check out something I had noticed hidden in a corner. It was a flat-topped, metal box, strategically positioned in an out-of-the-way space under the stairs. Eureka! A heating vent of some kind.

I strolled over and sat on it. Nothing. I waited. Nothing. I started to give up and leave when I suddenly heard a staccato set of clicking sounds. They were strange and non-rhythmic. Click. Click, click, click, click. Click, click. I sat there, eagerly anticipating. All at once, almost miraculously, hot air began to flow out of the vent slats. I was warm, deliriously and deliciously warm. I sat there for several minutes, under the stairs, in the dark, staring at a solo candle burning on a nearby altar. My head grew heavy and my body light. My soul seemed to levitate, and I experienced what may have been a deep mystical feeling. Or perhaps I just dozed off for a few minutes. Either way, it was divine.

Thereafter, on each winter evening when we visited the abbey, you could find me, in a similar "mystical" state, under the stairs in the back of the church. Sometimes the heater did not run, which was disappointing, but often it did. My relentless search for heat had an unexpected side effect. I came to cherish the stillness and solitude of a hushed and darkened winter space, illuminated solely by the flickering light of a single burning candle.

Mom felt differently. As winter drew near, she loudly announced to the amused monks that we would look forward to seeing them again in the springtime. Mom loathed even the thought of driving on snowy streets, which she referred to as "glare, glare ice," regardless of the amount of frozen water actually on the road. We could drive up a steep hill in the sweltering summer heat of July and she would immediately explain how unpleasant that hill would be to drive on in the snow. However, despite her occasional worries, the cold, and the high annual snowfall, we managed to visit the monastery in winter much more often than Mom had expected, and typically did so without incident.

During one trip, however, we found ourselves stuck in our car in a deep snowbank on the side of a mountain on a quiet and lonely Ogden Valley road. A major snowstorm was just ending, and the skies were as clear as an open window. It was beautiful outside, but it was treacherous. And it was nearing midnight. We should never have been out on such a road on such a night, but it was Christmas Eve. On Christmas Eve, we always went to Midnight Mass at the monastery. On the frosty night we got stuck, we felt compelled to try to attend Midnight Mass again, despite the big storm. So, we started the long drive from our apartment and up the narrow, two-lane road, thinking, *How bad can it be?* As we drove through the blizzard, snow flew horizontally at us, battering the windshield with frozen pellets and reducing driver visibility to just a few feet. Our windshield wipers struggled heroically to repulse the unrelenting snow, but we could not even see the road.

At one point, a few hundred yards past Pineview Dam, the car suddenly veered to the right, smashed into a patch of accumulated snow and ice, and started to skid. We careened sideways into the mountain and thudded to an abrupt stop. A wave of snow washed over us and covered half the car, a sort of meteorological exclamation point punctuating our plight. We sat there stunned. The only sound came from the car radio, which pretended that nothing had happened and continued to blissfully chirp out happy holiday tunes that praised the winter wonderland weather that entrapped us.

• Thomas Merton once said, "Happiness is not a matter of intensity but of balance, and order, and rhythm and harmony."[2] Trappist liturgies have a simple beauty, especially at midnight on a snowy Christmas Eve. But we were far away from that order and harmony, stuck in a mountainside snowbank, overlooking a frigid and foreboding Pineview Reservoir. If our car had slid the other way, we might have landed on, or more dreadfully in, the cold waters of that half-frozen lake. Because I was the "man" of the house, Mom and Karen immediately looked to me to help, but I did not have much to offer. By now a bit of a self-absorbed teenager, I was annoyed just to have to leave the warmth of our golden Ford Maverick to try to kick snow away from the back of the car to see if we could get moving again. As I made my half-hearted efforts, I berated my sister, who had been behind the wheel during the slide off, with a not-so-helpful comment, "What kind of driving was that?"

Just as it was becoming clear that I was not going to be able to rescue us from our plight, headlights appeared from out of the surrounding darkness.

They belonged to an old pickup truck, which in turn belonged to a grizzled old Huntsville farmer. He pulled next to us and rolled down his window. We shared a moment of fear and uncertainty until a friendly and distinctly Western voice cut through the cold air and asked, "You gals need some help?" Self-conscious (and male) teenager that I was, I hoped he was not referring to my long hair and instead was talking to my sister and mother, not to me. Perhaps sensing my embarrassment, Mom immediately responded, "Oh yes, please. Thank you!"

Our rescuer was tall, had a weathered face, and wore a denim jacket and worn leather gloves. Of course, he had on a cowboy hat. I do not remember his name or if he even shared that sort of information with us. He obviously was much better prepared for the storm than "us gals." He quickly pulled two snow shovels from his truck and kindly said, "Your boy can help me." Given his earlier greeting, I was relieved to hear my gender acknowledged. We shoveled away at the embankment of snow that had trapped our car. His snow flew farther and faster than mine, no doubt because I was in church shoes and he wore cowboy boots. He also put his back into the task. He got us out of the fix rather quickly, and soon our car was on the side of the road again, ready to continue its journey.

Mom thanked him, and tried to pay him, for his help. He politely declined, wished us well and left almost as quickly as he had appeared. I'd like to say he tipped his hat as he departed, but I don't remember for sure. We drove on to the monastery, uneventfully, and even made it there in time for Midnight Mass. The monks delivered their usual simple but impressive Christmas service. They had decorated their church with a Nativity scene, and a half dozen or so recently cut evergreen trees, one more than fifteen feet tall. Brother Isidore or Brother Carl, the forester monk, had probably hiked up the side of one of the Trappist foothills to obtain the lovely branches. White lights adorned a few of the trees, with the occasional addition of some simple red ribbons. The scent of fresh pine filled the chapel.

As bells rang out at midnight, the monks sang "Angels we have heard on high." The Christmas readings included the prophet Isaiah's poetic lines about the "Wonderful Counsellor, Mighty God, Everlasting Father, Prince of Peace," and Luke's lovely Gospel narrative of the Nativity.[3] At the end of Mass, the thirty or so monks raised their tenor and baritone voices in two or three verses of the classic carol "It Came Upon the Midnight Clear." This song, based on a poem written in 1849 by Massachusetts Unitarian pastor Edmund Sears, tells how in the darkest moment of Christmas Eve, the angels announced the birth of Jesus.

It was a most memorable night, but I probably only understood its significance years later, after I outgrew my teenage funk. The monks helped me to understand that, whether we celebrate it as a Christian holiday or not, the meaning of Christmas is that some 2,000 years ago, a force for peace, goodness, and joy was reintroduced into the world. Our task is to recognize and incarnate that force and give it meaning in the lives of our family, our friends and, as Charles Dickens once put it in *A Christmas Carol*, our "fellow passengers to the grave."

Several decades ago, on that snowy Christmas Eve near the small town of Huntsville, Utah, I think the Christ child came to my mother, my sister, and me. Instead of wearing swaddling clothes and lying in a manger, he arrived in leather gloves, cowboy boots, and an old pickup. And yes, he came upon a midnight clear.

■ ■ ■

CHAPTER 12

Monks and Saints

E ACH YEAR WITH THE THAW OF DEEP WINTER AT THE MONASTERY came the warmth of an approaching Easter. The hibernating mountain pasturelands and farms of Huntsville awoke and filled the three forks of the Ogden River with the icy cold runoff of the melting snowpack.

More than forty years after my first Easter at the monastery, the usually much-anticipated ritual of seasonal transformation and renewal felt different. It was 2017, and the last time the monks and the Saints would together welcome spring to the mountain valley they had shared for as long as anyone could remember.

Seventy years before, it was a spectacle—even a scandal—when three dozen Catholic monks settled into their new home in Mormon Utah. When the monks had arrived in 1947, the town was best known as the birthplace of David O. McKay, who soon would be president of the Church of Jesus Christ of Latter-day Saints.[1]

In separate news interviews during the monastery's golden anniversary celebration, Father Patrick and Brother Nicholas noted how the local community initially saw the monks' arrival as a threat.[2] Brother Nicholas said the monks' neighbors "were suspicious of men who never married, whose lives of farming and ranching were punctuated by chanted prayers seven times a day, beginning in the middle of the night."[3] The granddaughter of Huntsville's mayor recalled that the locals "were worried that something really bad was moving to Huntsville." Some even started a petition to try and force the Trappists out of the valley.[4]

The story of the monks and the Saints easily could have become another example of religious bigotry, strife, and intolerance. Instead, despite a few bumps along the road, it was a much different story.

The story started on a hopeful note. One of the pioneer monks who kept a travel log of the 1947 trip west noted, "Our life would not be understood by them [the Saints] but if we do well in agriculture here they will respect us."[5] Brother Boniface much more plainly explained what he expected from the monastery's neighbors when he first traveled west, that they would grow to like the monks because, "We could show our true face, show ourselves as we are—simple kids from different parts of the states."[6]

In their book *David O. McKay and the Rise of Modern Mormonism*, Gregory A. Prince and William Robert Wright (my former law partner) explain how relationships developed between the Latter-day Saint church and its neighboring denominations, including Catholics, in the 1940s and 1950s. The monastery unintentionally played an important role in that evolution.[7] Prince and Wright recount the challenges, advancements, and setbacks that occurred, particularly between McKay and Utah's fifth Catholic bishop, Duane G. Hunt. Their book, and a related article by Utah Catholic historian Gary Topping, tell how in 1953, an ad appeared in the *Wall Street Journal* soliciting funds to replace the existing temporary monastery building in Huntsville. This disturbed President McKay. The historians explain, "The monastery never engaged in proselytizing, yet McKay interpreted the campaign to build a new abbey as part of a campaign" to convert members of his church. McKay also was worried when he learned the monks were trying to buy more land in Huntsville. He expressed the concern that "the Catholic Church is against us."[8]

Events like this, and other related tensions, contributed to the decision by another local church leader, Elder Bruce R. McConkie, to refer to the Catholic Church as an "abomination" in his famous book *Mormon Doctrine*. McConkie was not alone in misjudging the other side. When the monks first arrived, they saw and heard a fire engine "racing down the main street, bell ringing and siren screaming." The monks had an interesting reaction: "There popped into our minds what Father Simon had said about Mormons killing the first '49ers who came through here during the gold rush. Ergo one frater [brother] was heard to breathe a deep sigh of relief when it [the fire truck] turned off before it reached us."[9]

McKay reportedly was "infuriated" by McConkie's book and the negative reference to the Catholic Church, which he had not seen beforehand.[10] President McKay and Bishop Hunt later discussed the book, as well as other aspects of their relationship, and as a result became friends, setting an ecumenical precedent that has been honored ever since by church presidents and Catholic bishops in Utah. When Hunt died in 1960, "McKay paid unprecedented respect to the bishop by attending his funeral Mass at the Cathedral of the Madeleine."[11] The new Catholic bishop, Joseph Lennox Federal, returned the favor and attended the funeral services in the tabernacle when McKay died in 1970. Moreover, as McKay's funeral procession passed the Cathedral of the Madeleine, "on its slow, sad journey along South Temple Street to the Salt Lake City cemetery, [Federal] ordered its bells tolled in a final demonstration of respect."[12]

Following this example, when the monks got to Huntsville they did not criticize or bother the Saints, or try to change them, or take over the small town. The Saints left the strangers to the hard work of building a productive farm and community from what had been an uncultivated ranch. Moment by moment, person by person, the monks and the Saints cautiously connected with each other, sometimes on business matters, but typically on the often mundane things about which neighbors interact. They got to know each other, and the rest took care of itself.

As the monk who worked most frequently outside the abbey to sell the monastery's products, Brother Felix led the community outreach. Father Patrick once joked that if Brother Felix had not been a monk, he would have been elected Huntsville's mayor. Brother Felix befriended those concerned about the monks' arrival, as well as Mayor Abner Allen. He even spoke at Mayor Allen's funeral. Another Huntsville resident told how when Brother Felix heard that her husband had died in a plane crash, he spontaneously appeared at her door and told her to call him if she needed anything.[13] On another occasion, when a farmer suffered a back injury at harvest time, the monks showed up at his farm, harvested some of his crops for him, and irrigated his fields. The monks also donated land so Huntsville could build a water treatment facility. Indeed, from my days there, I recall the monks only speaking fondly of their neighbors.[14]

The good feelings were mutual. Some young Latter-day Saint men spent time in contemplation and retreat at the monastery in preparation for their church missions. The Saints took good care of the Trappist neighbors they once had feared.[15] During their first winter in Huntsville in 1947–48, one neighborly farmer each week brought over supplies of wheat and milk to help get the newcomers through to their first full planting and growing season. The monks responded by building and presenting the neighbor with a lovely grandfather clock. For years, volunteers at the quaint, one-room Huntsville Historical Library have lovingly collected and maintained detailed scrapbooks about the monks and the monastery. The Huntsville Latter-day Saint ward supplied food, tables, and chairs for many events there, including funerals and a reception after the installation of one of the new abbots. James McKay, a member of the ward, and Huntsville's mayor, said of the monks: "It's a blessing for us to have them in our community."[16]

At some point, the abbey's bakery equipment failed, and the monks did not have the resources to replace it or continue to bake their own famous bread. A friend of the monastery, Horace Snyder, heard that one of the Latter-day Saint bakeries was undergoing renovations and replacing its equipment.[17] The Latter-day Saints operate an extensive welfare operation to assist those in need. Snyder told church bakery officials about the monastery's predicament and facilitated their visit to the abbey. They decided that their old equipment would work just fine there and could be installed and used at the abbey. Bakery manager Jim Blake personally supervised the installation at the abbey and "soon the monks were again enjoying fresh-baked bread."[18]

The warm relationship between the monks and their neighbors reached an unusual, but delightful, final chapter during the last year the monastery was open. Each Fourth of July, Huntsville holds an old-fashioned Independence Day celebration, with most festivities occurring beneath the shade of towering old trees in the town park. Activities include a flag-raising ceremony, a pancake breakfast, pie-eating contests, musical performances, fireworks and, of course, a parade.

The parade is vintage red, white, and blue Americana, filled with hundred-year-old tractors and children throwing saltwater taffy from family-decorated floats. In 2017, the last year of the monastery, three

Monks and Saints 109

ninety-year-old Utah monks joined the classic promenade, serving as grand marshals of the parade. They wore straw hats or festive ball caps to protect them from the blazing sun and rode in a horse-drawn buggy. As they circled the park, hundreds of Huntsville Saints rose from their seats, shook the monks' hands, waved, and clapped for their Catholic neighbors. It was a touching final moment of friendship between peoples with very different belief systems.

Such has not always been the case in Utah. A Catholic growing up in or moving to Utah is part of a distinct minority group, and this status sometimes can create problems. In Utah, the gulf between Latter-day Saints and others has been called the "Unspoken Divide," but that divide actually is spoken of frequently.[19] In 2001, *The Salt Lake Tribune* researched and published an extensive and detailed report about it.[20] One participant in a community project aimed at bridging the divide described it this way: "Salt Lake City is like the South was. This town is divided, except it is divided by religious affiliation rather than skin color. It controls who we hang out with. Who we date. Who we marry. But I would never say it out loud."[21]

Catholics often react in different ways to the minority role thrust upon them. Many adapt just fine and make friendly social, business, and other connections with their neighbors. Some experience segregation and exclusion, such as neighbors who do not want their kids to associate with children of a different religion. Others choose to associate only with those who share their faith, essentially confining themselves to a Catholic ghetto. Some make unkind comments about the Saints. As the Huntsville monks and their neighbors have demonstrated, it takes two sides to disagree and two sides to work to overcome possible disagreements. Catholics need to be reminded of this important point just as much as Latter-day Saints.

One of the best reminders for me came from our 1970s Ogden parish priest, Father John LaBranche. Our home was just two blocks from the second-oldest parish in Utah, St. Joseph's Catholic Church, which sits prominently on a hill overlooking downtown. Its church building is one of the most splendid in the state, made of beautiful red-and-tan stone and highlighted by several wondrous stained glass windows dedicated in 1902 under the watchful eye of founding pastor Monsignor Patrick

Cushnahan, originally from County Donegal, Ireland. The huge white wooden front altarpiece, dating from 1905, is a Gothic masterpiece, consisting of a half dozen or so separate intricate and hand-carved towers. The church is a historical landmark.

Father LaBranche, ordained in 1940, was a short, stocky, pleasant, and perpetually red-faced man from a devout Catholic family in Ely, Nevada. Both of his sisters became nuns. He wore thick glasses and a flattop haircut like a marine. Both spiritual and practical, he could run a parish, preach the gospel, teach religion and theology classes, and repair and drive the school bus when needed. He had a wicked sense of humor, once instructing me that the best way to make holy water was to put a pan of water on the stove and boil the hell out of it. Father LaBranche also acted as a therapist of sorts, a kind listening ear for me and a classmate whose parents also had recently been divorced. During several impromptu sessions after he taught our seventh-grade religion class, he would ask how I was doing, listen patiently to any recent divorce-related dustups, and offer suggestions or advice. Most often, he would just share a kind word or a joke to make me laugh and feel a little better.

My friendship with Father LaBranche, short but sweet, helped me understand that priests are human beings with fears, hopes, and longings, just like the rest of us. He contracted cancer and seemed to have recovered, but he had glimpsed into the end-of-life abyss. His brush with death provoked him one day to tell me, although he was not that old, that he hoped he would not die alone. Some omnipotent Being must have heard that wish, and granted it, to thank him for his many kindnesses to many people. When he did pass away from heart failure in 1977 at age 63, he was with several close friends on a fishing-and-camping trip. We were told that his final words were: "Sweet Jesus, how good it is to be so close to you!"

A few years before that untimely passing, Father LaBranche conveyed an ecumenical lesson to us after an unfortunate incident at a Christmas interfaith worship session in December 1974 at the Tabernacle adjacent to the Ogden Latter-day Saint Temple. The St. Joseph's Elementary School choir was invited to participate in the service. I was an alto in the choir. I did not really know what it meant to be an alto, so I just sang what I wanted, which probably was melody in a low voice. Our choir director either did not notice or did not mind my not-so-alto tones. We attended the Christmas service and sang an Italian folk carol called "O Bambino." My favorite part was when we got to sing a few words in Italian. We sang well, the audience liked us, and we resumed our seats to a healthy round of applause.

Afterward, the host introduced Father LaBranche and we cheered, way too loudly. It was a pep rally-like cheer that was inappropriate for the setting. The host smiled and told Father LaBranche he had a lot of friends. Father LaBranche strained to smile, raised his index finger and pointed to heaven, and said "just one." Some students made snide comments about Mormons that some in the audience overheard. Father LaBranche later told us, politely but firmly, that he thought we were way out of line and that we had embarrassed him and ourselves. He said we had disrespected our hosts. While acknowledging that we were a minority in Utah, he explained that we needed to learn better, kinder, and more tolerant ways to relate to those who held religious views different from ours. It was one of those "grow up kid" messages that good teachers sometimes must give their students.

I do not know how many of my fellow Catholic choir boys and choir girls recall his words or tried to take them to heart. I remember the life lesson all too well and I have tried to apply it and grow from it. Father LaBranche's words, and the example of the monks and the Saints, taught me to build bridges with my neighbors rather than focus on the religious rivers that might keep us on opposing banks.

Any brief exposure to the news of the day, describing a world often ripped apart by various forms of intolerance, including religious bias, confirms that this is one of those basic lessons we all must learn young, and then learn again on a regular basis. We should try, like the monks and the Saints, to build friendships measured not in days, months, or even years, but in decades.

■ ■ ■

CHAPTER 13

Fellow Pilgrims Seeking Light

P ERHAPS LIKE MANY OTHER CONSECRATED PLACES, THE MONASTERY attracted people who were interested in monks, but not necessarily interested in becoming monks. The Utah Trappists welcomed them all, abiding by the Rule of St. Benedict, which mandates, "All guests to the monastery should be welcomed as Christ, because He will say, 'I was a stranger and you took me in.'"[1] Many such guests were sightseers or simply curious. Some possibly were a little bit crazy. Most were just like us, like Mom and me, searching for a still point in a turning world that seemed to have spun out of control. We all were pilgrims seeking the light in our own ways. Collectively, we formed an interesting and important subset of the larger monastic community.

For a time, the monastery acted as a parish of sorts for the Catholics who lived in the Huntsville area. The Catholic diocese eventually built St. Florence's Church in the Ogden Valley, but not until 1990. Before then, the monks offered a Sunday Mass every week for their Catholic neighbors. For a couple of years, Mom and my sister Karen taught a youth catechism class, held at and supported by the abbey, for about a half-dozen children, some of them farming families. This led to new friendships. One local family, the Sansones, befriended us and hosted a brunch for me before I left for college. Not surprising for fine Italian Catholics transplanted from the Chicago area, they even served me wine at the brunch.

Kind pilgrims visiting the abbey also shared interesting, and very Catholic, gifts with us. We never really traveled anywhere outside of Utah, but we lived vicariously through the many travelers who wandered the world and then arrived at the monastery and told us about their journeys.

One such gift was an olive tree leaf from the Garden of Gethsemane in Jerusalem, the site where Jesus prayed the night before his crucifixion. The inscription on the card to which the leaf is attached explains, "In the Garden of Gethsemane, guarded with love by the Franciscans, there are still eight venerable olive trees, witnesses of the painful agony of the Redeemer. Their leaves are esteemed by pious pilgrims and faithful Christians as precious souvenirs."

An even more amazing and strange gift was a small piece of bone from the body of St. Clare of Assisi, who died in 1253. Like her friend St. Francis, St. Clare was a rock star in our home, and it is amazing to think that our family has owned such a venerated object that is well over 700 years old. The relic includes a certificate of authenticity signed and dated January 10, 1968, from the Office of the Vicar General of Rome, led at that time by Cardinal Luigi Traglia. As a child, I thought it odd that if you were revered or sainted in the Catholic Church, your deceased body was at imminent risk of being chopped up and distributed to the faithful piece by piece. The practice seems less strange to me now, as a parent, because I treasure relics from the younger ages of our children, such as a first tooth or a lock of hair.

Many of the people we encountered at Holy Trinity Abbey were suffering. For a time, an older man who had restlessly traveled most of the world alone lived in the guest quarters for several months, until he then left again. I never knew his full story, but I suspect he was wandering in search of peace and meaning. I also remember several visits to the monastery by a young, tall, thin woman with long brown hair who told us her body was riddled with arthritis. She struggled just to walk and did so in obvious pain. I was confused that someone so young would have arthritis, which I had assumed only afflicted older people. As a Catholic growing up on stories of miraculous cures occurring at far-off places such as Lourdes and Fatima, I wondered if the abbey air or water might miraculously cure her. I hope it did.

I also remember "Terrific Tim," as he called himself. He was a former boxer who came to Utah by way of Chicago and New York and went by Timothy Francis O'Rourke, which also was not his real name. He told us "Terrific Tim" was his fighting name. You could tell by his face, and his perpetually swollen red nose, that he may have taken a punch or two, either in the ring or elsewhere. He was a short and stocky Irishman, missing a few teeth, and solidly built, but his once barrel-like chest had sunk into a pot belly by the time we met him. You could hear Terrific Tim coming, even from a distance. He had a clumsy and heavy gait, and he walked downstairs primarily with his weight on the back of his heels, resulting in a loud clump, clump, clump on each descent. He loved to sing, laughed easily, and his voice was loud and husky, seasoned no doubt by many cigarettes and shots of whiskey.

There must have been many shots of whiskey, because I believe he was visiting Holy Trinity Abbey in his sixties, trying to deal with the ravages resulting from an apparently lifelong struggle with alcoholism. In Ogden, he moved around. He lived in various low-income boarding houses and used to frequent a place called the Alano Club, affiliated with Alcoholics Anonymous. I liked him a lot, and we would often work together in the bookstore and the chicken coop. I do not know for certain, but I suspect now that the monks gave him some financial aid as well as spiritual support, guidance, and simple friendship. I think Mom sympathetically saw her alcoholic father in him. At what must have been one particularly bad stretch of time, he lived for several days in an extra room we had in our apartment. He was the first homeless person I knew.

All in all, a colorful cast of people visited the monastery, and we added our own unique tones to the monastic mural. When I think about these faces now, I see many breaking or broken people—like us—all searching for hope and healing. The monks took us all in, each pilgrim arriving in Huntsville at a critical point in life and seeking their own unique guidance and light. Light: we often take it for granted, but there is no life without light. Light surrounds us, both literally and figuratively. In nature, we bask in the sun, we love by the moon, and we dream by the stars. In language, we are enlightened, people brighten our days, we hear glowing reports, and we beam with delight. In philosophy, we acknowledge that it is better to light a single candle than to curse the darkness. Light is especially important at Christmastime, the season of light, when the winter solstice gives us the shortest day of the year, the day Mom was born.

I recall a memorable moment of light from our days visiting the Monastery. We were friends with a large family, seven or eight kids. They also had a Chihuahua, or at least that is what I think it was. I never actually saw the little beast, but it would snarl and growl, viciously and endlessly, and never come out from underneath the couch in their home. They visited the monastery, too, but without the miniature hound from hell. They lived in a small and run-down house in a back alley, slept several people to a room, and once told me they reused the same bath water after one of them had finished in the tub. They must have been low income like us. With so many playmates and so little time, however, I never paid much attention to such economic details back then. I never lingered on the tearful moments when their mother might be telling my mom about their financial troubles, about bills unpaid and creditors calling.

One day, around Christmastime, Mom and I strolled over to Utah Power and Light, the electric utility company with an office just around the corner from the apartment where we lived. This was odd indeed. We mailed in our payment. I knew this because I usually got to lick the stamps. We walked into the office, and I heard Mom tell the clerk she was there to pay our friends' electric bill, now several months overdue. She wrote a check, handed it to the clerk, and we left. I did not fully understand home economics, but I knew Mom struggled mightily to pay the many bills for her own family. I asked, "Why are you paying someone else's electric bill?" She smiled and said, "To help them." I doubt that she ever told our friends who had paid their power bill during the holidays.

For many years I had heard priests, deacons, monks, homilists, preachers, and teachers spend long hours trying to explain to me the meaning of Matthew's Gospel (5:14–16) admonition: "You are the light of the world. A city set on a hill cannot be hid. Nor do men light a lamp and put it under a bushel, but on a stand, and it gives light to all in the house. Let your light so shine before men, that they may see your good works and give glory to your Father who is in heaven." On the day she paid someone else's electricity bill, Mom never mentioned a word about God or gospel, but at last, I understood.

■ ■ ■

CHAPTER 14

Discordant Notes in the Choir

T HOMAS MERTON WROTE THAT THE "SOUL OF A MONK IS BETHLEHEM where Christ comes to be born."[1] He just as easily could have explained that the soul of a monk is Calvary where Christ comes to suffer and be crucified. Life in a monastery certainly is not easy. Monks and priests, like the rest of us, are imperfect souls. They err, sometimes they do not keep their promises to God or to each other, and sometimes they even enter monasteries by mistake. Merton thought these monastic imperfections were smaller than those found outside a monastery "and yet somehow you tend to notice them more and feel them more, because they get to be so greatly magnified." Said another way, again according to Merton, "People even lose their vocations because they find out that a man can spend forty or fifty or sixty years in a monastery and still have a bad temper."[2] I guess what he really meant is not at all surprising—priests, monks, and nuns are flawed humans too.

The story of Merton and his Utah book censor may best illustrate his point. Fr. Thomas Aquinas Porter, as I've mentioned, was one of our monk friends. For a time, he locked the monastery doors at the end of the evening chant, called Compline. We often attended Compline and enjoyed many pleasant conversations with him afterwards. He had a kind face, salt and pepper hair, and a quick, loud, infectious laugh. He passed away in 1997. I should have suspected that he was an accomplished scholar too. It was only many years later (in fact, only when I was writing this book) that I learned that Father Thomas also served as one of Merton's official censors. As a monk, Merton had to submit his writings for approval by designated readers within the Cistercian order who would comment on the draft and/or suggest changes. Although I never had the chance to discuss this intriguing relationship with my Utah friend, Merton actually wrote about it in 1956.

Editing relationships can be challenging, and apparently, in the course of some back and forth about one of his works (*Basic Principles of Monastic Spirituality*), some feelings were hurt. I have not yet read Father Thomas's side of the correspondence, but Merton's letters relating to the incident appear in *The School of Charity*, edited by Brother Patrick Hart. The issue eventually reached the head of the order in Rome, who, as Merton put it, "lays this at my door." Merton apologized by letter to Father Thomas on August 27, 1956, saying that others told him, "I was much more aggressive than I realized," and thus, "I deeply regret if I have wounded you." Merton urged Father Thomas to continue serving as his censor and even included with the apology letter more of his writing for Father Thomas to review.[3]

Noting that "authors and censors inevitably tangle once in a while," Merton stated, "An author, certainly a Trappist author, is always eager to comply with the censor, but at the same time, when the correction affects some very minute point and involves perhaps a mere matter of opinion, the author would like a little freedom so as to spare his text from the sort of mutilation involved by the forcible injection of a technical phrase." One week later, Merton wrote a similar letter to Dom Gabriel Sortais, the head of the Cistercians at the time. He explained that despite the practice of anonymous review, he had detected in the editing what he called the "style of good Father Thomas Aquinas in Utah" and had written to him seeking to eliminate certain imposed corrections that the other censors had not deemed necessary. Merton repeated to Dom Gabriel what he had said directly to Father Thomas: "I deeply regret I have hurt him." He concluded, "I know I am not a saint" but "I do hope that I am going to make some progress with God's grace."[4]

I knew Father Thomas as a kind, thoughtful, dedicated monk. He was well regarded in the order and served in transitional leadership roles at other monasteries to assist them as needed. I am sure he dedicated himself to the censor role with a sense of duty, responsibility, and zeal. Therein may be the source of the conflict. Merton's letters called him "scrupulous" but also "demanding." Merton said Father Thomas made him feel "unnecessarily cramped," but also noted that his censor worked with "great care." Their stressful encounter may have been the result of a gifted right-brained author meeting a gifted left-brained censor.

Although such natural tension between human beings with differing points of view probably was common in Utah, as elsewhere, I can only think of a few occasions when I personally heard of or witnessed discord at, or related to, the monastery. These occasions involved a grumpy gatekeeper, a self-proclaimed street prophet, a dog, a less-than-hospitable monk, and psychological counseling.

A gatekeeper who was not a monk closed and locked the exterior monastery gate each night at 8 p.m. I do not know what his real name was, but everyone called him "Smitty," so I assume his name was something like "John Smith." I did not know Smitty well, but during our limited interactions he never impressed me as a joyful soul. Perhaps he had his reasons. I thought this was odd, because it seemed like he had a great gig: married, living in a nice house at the lovely monastery, possibly rent free, and working with the monks.

Sometimes after the Compline evening service, which ended at about 7:45 p.m., we would visit with one or more of the monks. I enjoyed these visits. Mom loved these visits too, but they also caused her great stress. She would glance repeatedly at her watch, worried that we would not make it down Abbey Road and out of the monastery grounds before Smitty locked the gate. She did not want to upset or disrespect the gatekeeper or the monks as a result.

Although we had a few close calls, we only got locked in once. It was a long (and, from my perspective, quite fun) visit with a monk that delayed us, and the monk delaying us did not seem to be worried about it either. However, Mom was nervous and told Karen to "step on it" as soon as we got into the car. We raced down Abbey Road. Alas, as we got to the end of the road, we saw that the gate was already locked. I liked the idea of being locked in, but Mom most certainly did not. She had to walk over to Smitty's house, knock on the door, and humbly ask him to let us out. He did so, but was not happy with us, perhaps rightfully so, although it was not clear he had any other pressing obligations. Mom was not happy either. It was a long, quiet ride home.

These locked gates were mild trouble compared with a potentially deranged former monk wandering around town. One such unhinged person, associated with the abbey in its early days, was Brother Pascal. I found out later he was known to his peers as "Pascal the rascal." He had a rough early life, losing both parents and a brother during the 1918 Spanish flu epidemic and growing up in orphanages. After he left the monastery, he made an infamous name for himself in downtown Ogden as "Dominic the prophet." He took on the identity of an Old Testament ascetic and wandered the streets dressed in mostly white robes and carrying a large stick. He was unkempt, his hair was tangled, his eyes were wild, and he would yell at strangers and spout biblical condemnations. According to court and newspaper records, his behavior also became sexually inappropriate. Local prosecutors charged and convicted him of several criminal offenses in the mid-1970s. One judge sternly warned Dominic that he would only avoid jail time if he limited his "outbreaks" and stopped "getting in people's hair."[5]

There did not seem to be anything negative, at least at first, about the fact that during our early visits to Holy Trinity Abbey, they had a dog on the farm. He was a huge, friendly, and rambunctious Saint Bernard named Fritz, and seemed to be especially close to the irrigation manager, Father Alan Hohl. A Saint Bernard seemed liked the perfect dog for the Trappists, given the breed's reputation for working with Swiss monks and carrying miniature kegs of brandy for weary travelers, and given that one of the greatest of the Trappists was named St. Bernard of Clairvaux.

I liked Fritz a lot, but then one day he was gone. Someone told us that abbey authorities had concluded monks should not have pets and that the dog was an obstacle to the monastic life. The real story, however, was that poor Fritz and a canine friend named Spandau got too fond of chasing sheep, a game ended by a local sheep rancher's rifle. Thereafter, the Utah Trappists kept cats, which controlled the mice better anyway.

There was only one time I ever felt unwanted at the abbey. During one visit, I decided to make my way to the small cemetery and visit Brother Ferdinand's grave. I looked at the other white crosses for the monks I did not know, said a short prayer for Brother Ferdinand, and started to leave. This time, however, I got caught. I noticed a novice, Brother Yaroslav, watching me. He waved me over to where he sat and asked who I prayed for, and I told him. He praised me for the prayer, and then politely but firmly told me that while I had done a good deed, I was trespassing in the private area for the monks and should not be there. He was not rude, and he was absolutely correct. Still, I cannot help wondering how Brother Boniface or Father Patrick or Father David might have handled the situation differently.

I also was sad when I heard that the monastery had required one of the brothers, who seemed fine and whom I quite liked, to undergo psychological counseling. I never knew the reasons, but that monk did so willingly and obediently and remained at the abbey his entire life. Such counseling carried an unfortunate stigma in the 1970s, but now seems like an entirely healthy thing to do, even for a monk. In fact, I'm told that it is now routine for men to receive similar testing before they are allowed to make their final vows. But this is further proof that the Trappist brothers were human, and that the problems confronted by those of us in outside secular life do not just vanish when one puts on a monk's robes, passes through a monastery's doors, and enters into its solitude.

Father David Altman, eventually an abbot at Holy Trinity, has explained that in "a monastery, there is little or no escape. The monk must put forth great effort to make many relationships work and to grow through them." He also compared monastic life to a marriage, "where the primary focus is on efforts to make relationships work, and this is challenging work."[6] Sometimes, however, both inside and outside a monastery, the relationships do not work, or they get supplanted by other relationships. The first time I saw this happen in the religious life involved different paths taken by two friends associated with Holy Trinity Abbey, Brother Isidore and Father Charles Cummins.

Father Cummins, not to be confused with the monastery's monk/priest named Father Charles Cummings, was commonly known as Father Chuck. He was a tall, dark, handsome, Warren Beatty look-alike from New Jersey. He had degrees in business accounting and philosophy, served as a Marine Corps officer for four years, and became a priest in 1968. He was a certified pilot and scuba diver. When we first met him at the monastery, a visitor to the place just like us, he was in his mid-thirties, wore a moustache, and had been a priest for less than ten years. He was working in Salt Lake City as a hospital chaplain.

Like the monastery's Father Manny, Father Chuck previously had attended the seminary in, and served as a priest for, the Archdiocese of Los Angeles. What exactly brought him to Holy Trinity I do not know, but he stayed for quite a while, and even helped Father Alan with the irrigation after the monk had neck surgery and wore a neck brace just below his shaved head. One day in the fields, a visitor asked Father Chuck what had happened to Father Alan, who was standing a few feet away. Father Chuck responded, "Oh him? He just had a head transplant, but for the life of me I don't know why he didn't get one with hair."

He loved to joke, but when I first met him Father Chuck may have been pondering his future and the direction of his life. Perhaps he even was considering whether he should continue to be a priest. Given his obvious good looks, I'd be shocked if he did not have other tempting offers that did not involve celibacy. This is all a boy's speculation. I never discussed any of this with him. We did make small talk and discuss athletics, because he was a huge sports fan.

Once while Father Chuck was visiting the abbey, someone left a note with a poem on it in our car. I still remember the poem because it included a word I had never seen before and rarely saw afterward: "Elected Silence, sing to me, / And beat upon my whorled ear." The new vocabulary word was "whorled." I later learned it means something in a spiraled or twisted shape. I always wanted to use whorled in a sentence (and just did). The poem was the "Habit of Perfection," written in 1866 by the English poet Gerard Manley Hopkins. Hopkins became a Catholic and then a Jesuit priest shortly after he wrote it. The story of Hopkins's conversion prompted Thomas Merton to become a Catholic. I learned all this later, but what a coincidence to be at a Trappist monastery and receive a poem written by the man who basically sent one of the most famous Trappists ever on his path to a monastery.[7]

The poem pays homage to the contemplative life by describing how it is lived in terms of each of the senses (hearing, sight, etc.). The use of *habit* in the title seems to be a play on words, referring at once to what a monk wears and to what a monk does. The first verse of the poem describes silence beating on a "whorled" ear, much like a loud burst of music would do. The image of silence as music, indeed as "the music that I care I hear," is simply excellent. We wondered, but never confirmed, whether the poem was a gift from Father Chuck, perhaps his way of acknowledging our shared mutual respect and affection for the monastery and the monks. Today, I wonder if the word "whorled" stood out to me because it symbolically described the twisting spirals of doubt and emotion that may have been rocking the worlds of both Father Chuck and Brother Isidore as they tried to discern their true vocations, something I could not possibly comprehend as the young boy who knew and liked them.

Brother Isidore was a large, charismatic, handsome man with a shining face, and black hair with graying temples. He was full of life and vigor. We saw him often and he insisted that we call him "Izzy" and sometimes, with a twinkle in his eye, referred to himself as "Isidorable." With his high energy, he must have been the perfect monk to work on a farm. He joined Holy Trinity Abbey right after high school in 1951. He was a Sullivan (originally named Charles) with a twin brother, from Casper, Wyoming. At Holy Trinity, he took on the name Isidore, possibly after the patron saint for farmers. He had a natural Irish clannish affinity for anyone named O'Brien, but even more so for us, after he learned that we also had Sullivans in our family tree.[8]

Father Chuck and Brother Isidore seemed to be good friends. We saw them together often. They were about the same age. They both were big, strong, gregarious men and worked together on the farm. I suspect they talked to each other a lot too, possibly about their lives and their futures. We have a striking photo of them together, quite handsome in their full religious garbs. They both are smiling. Brother Isidore is in his black-and-white Trappist robes and Father Chuck in his ankle-length, black, priestly cassock. I am glad we took this picture when we did, because soon thereafter it would have been impossible to do so.

Sometime in 1974, we noticed Brother Isidore was nowhere to be seen, not in church, not in the fields, not anywhere. Given how often and how regularly we had seen him on previous visits, this was odd, and we worried about him. When we asked about him, the other monks were appropriately discreet. The most specific update we got from anyone was that he was taking a personal leave of absence. One evening, the doorbell rang at our apartment. It was Brother Isidore, in street clothes. None of the monks ever had visited our home before, nor did any of them do so afterward. This was also one of the rare occasions I saw one of them in regular clothes. We invited him in.

Unfortunately, it was an awkward visit. He told us that he needed to do something different with his life. He had developed a relationship with a woman who had been visiting the monastery. He said he loved the abbey and his brother monks, but he was confused and needed time to consider what he wanted to do, and how he was meant to best serve God and live his life. It was the first time that I witnessed directly the agonized circumstance of a professed priest or monk leaving that clerical mantle behind. Izzy came to us looking for friendship, support, and perhaps even guidance as he did so.

I regret that he did not get it from us. I was sad my buddy was leaving the abbey. Mom was still fresh off her own divorce. Having so recently experienced one man walking away from his vows and promises to her, I do not think she was, or even could be, sympathetic to Brother Isidore as he was walking away from his vows and his two decades at the monastery, no matter how good the reasons for doing so. Our visit with him was not mean or angry or ugly, and no accusatory words were exchanged, but I remember it being difficult and uncomfortable. It broke a bond between us. I do not know if it had to work out that way, but that is how it worked out.

Later, we briefly discussed this with Father Chuck, and he strongly admonished us that only Brother Isidore could decide how God was calling him to live his life. Isidore did leave the monastery for good. In 1975, he married the woman with whom he had fallen in love. We saw them occasionally afterward at the abbey and exchanged polite small talk. Taking a different path, Father Chuck remained a priest and took up residence in Ogden, serving as a chaplain for both the student Newman Center at Weber State University and for the nearby St. Benedict's Hospital. He also was a teacher, coach, and the Huntsville Catholic parish/mission pastor.[9]

From what I later learned about Izzy, he lived a good, decent, honest, and productive life away from the monastery. He was a devoted husband for forty years. He worked hard at many different jobs, was a kind stepfather and a loving grandfather, and stayed in close touch with Brother Nicholas at the abbey, whom he described as his "best friend."[10]

The Rule of St. Benedict prescribes stern treatment for a brother who leaves a monastery, stating that to return, he must "first promise the complete amending of the fault," and then he will be received back, "but in the lowest rank, so his humility may be put to the test."[11] The Utah monks were far more kind to Izzy, who visited the monastery regularly over the years after he left, volunteering to do various chores to help them. One news reporter observed Izzy at another monk's funeral, thirty years after Izzy had left Holy Trinity, and described how his eyes were fixed on the altar where the monks stood. As the monks prayed, the reporter said Izzy "was sitting low, slightly hunched, praying, and chanting in time, word for word. Just like them."[12]

Sometimes there are discordant notes in the choir, but they too are part of the music of life. I hope Isidore and Father Chuck both found happiness and contentment after the time I knew them as a boy. Watching, even from a distance, as they seemed to grapple with their life decisions left an indelible mark on me. It was a vivid lesson about how we all try to find happiness and serve God and each other in unique ways and in different places, about how we stumble, fall, and get up again as we walk along our own individual rocky life paths. Maybe this is why the gospel warns us about casting stones at others?

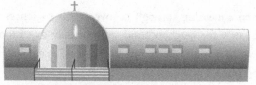

CHAPTER 15

The Unwanted Lineup

Aᴌᴛʜᴏᴜɢʜ I ᴇɴᴊᴏʏᴇᴅ ᴍʏ ѕᴄʜᴏᴏʟ ᴅᴀʏѕ, ѕᴜᴍᴍᴇʀᴛɪᴍᴇ ᴡᴀѕ ʙᴇᴛᴛᴇʀ. I loved the warm and dry mountain desert summers of my middle school years before high school. We had moved from Clearfield to Ogden so Mom could be closer to her job. Ogden was the second largest city in Utah, ranking behind only Salt Lake City in terms of population and prestige. Mom and Karen both worked during the long summer days, so I was the sole occupant and master of the house from roughly nine to five from June through August. This left me largely unfettered and free to explore and rule our castle and its surrounding realms.

The castle was an upstairs, two-bedroom, 1,000-square-foot apartment. Everything I needed was within a four- to five-block radius. Downtown Ogden's stores and parks were but a block away, and St. Joseph's Church was within two blocks. If I traveled two-and-a-half blocks I found the Weber County Library, a beloved haven where I spent several hours a day exploring the shelves, reading magazines in the periodicals section, and listening to tapes in the audio-visual room. Near the library was the Deseret Gymnasium, where I could meet my friends to play basketball, jump on trampolines, or swim. And within three blocks of our apartment was the Grand Central store, part of a chain of Utah discount department stores where I disposed of the small amounts of cash I had available, typically at either the candy counter or the bakery.

I traversed intrepidly through these various venues of early teen life on my trusty bicycle, the one with the ultra-cool banana seat and the distinctive high handlebars. I learned all the back roads and shortcuts of the area, blazed a few new trails of my own, and used them all regularly, sometimes even squeezing through or over walls or fences with my bike in tow. I knew the neighborhood so intimately that I took on the afternoon newspaper route, delivering *The Ogden Standard-Examiner* to homes and apartments in the area.

The neighborhood was not especially dangerous or menacing, but it was an aging, low-income, high-density urban district with mixed commercial and residential property. In my mind, I was nothing short of immortal. I was blissfully ignorant of any of the risks. In fact, my summer freedom and perceived dominance of my world were so intoxicating and confidence-building that I eventually ventured back into a world where I had previously enjoyed only mixed success—competitive sports. In the summer of 1975, I joined a Little League baseball team that practiced and played at a ballpark five blocks from our home.

I first developed an interest in baseball while watching the underdog New York Mets, the "Miracle Mets," win the 1969 World Series. This miracle made us baseball fans. My sister Karen and I also watched Roberto Clemente and the Pittsburgh Pirates win the 1971 World Series, later admiring how Clemente sacrificed himself in a plane crash while bringing relief supplies to the victims of a massive earthquake in Nicaragua. We attended several minor league games of the Ogden Dodgers, the rookie-level farm baseball team. Our team played in the Pioneer League, at a rickety old wooden stadium called John Affleck Park near the railroad tracks on the industrial west side. It was a ramshackle setting the team typically outshined. Hall of Fame coach and Los Angeles Dodger legend Tommy Lasorda coached them to several Pioneer League championships in the 1960s. His players included future major leaguers such as Steve Garvey, Bill Buckner, and Bobby Valentine.[1]

My previous adventures in Little League were unremarkable. In third grade, I signed up for the Catholic league. I played for the Robins, a nice enough team name that did not strike much fear into the hearts of our opponents. The coach made me the shortstop, which was amusing and ironic because half of the ground balls hit my way shot right past my mitt or skidded between my legs. I was a better batter, but only because I was smart enough to figure out that very few pitchers in the league threw strikes. Most of the time I stood at the plate and let them walk me. I was happy to get on base, but my method frustrated my family—although I think the movie *Moneyball* later vindicated my just-get-on-base tactics! They started loudly urging me to "swing" during those frequent at bats when I stood there and watched the balls fly by. One time I followed their loud advice and struck out.

Middle-school baseball was different. The pitchers were more accurate, and out of necessity, I started swinging at (and even hitting) some pitches. I was not a bad fielder either. The coach noticed my efforts and my playing time increased. One momentous evening after practice, as the summer season was ending, the coach told me he had to submit a lineup for the league all-star team and he was considering adding my name to the proposed list. The sun had just set and my chest swelled with pride as I rode my trusty bike home. I was dazzled by the exciting prospects of being included in such an esteemed lineup.

Little did I know that I was destined instead to participate in a much different kind of—and unwanted—lineup.

After practice, I was riding down the hill on 26th Street, about a block from home, when I veered left to take one of my shortcuts. It was through the parking lot of an abandoned building, a former luxurious mansion used for many years as a wedding reception center. It was called "The White House" or something like that. My shortcut would take me through the parking lot, past and over a low wall and fence, and into the back area of the Towne Apartments complex where we lived. There usually was no one there, but this time was different.

As I entered the dark parking lot, a man suddenly appeared in front of me. He surprised me and walked quickly up to the bike and firmly took hold of the handlebars. He was fairly large, certainly larger than me, and wore dark glasses and a hat pulled down to partially conceal his face. He asked me where he could find Harrison Boulevard, which was several blocks away. Trying to be helpful, I started to tell him and point the way, when he suddenly maneuvered behind the bike and straddled the back of it. I was starting to feel uneasy about the situation.

My unease quickly turned into terror when he forced the bike into some bushes on the side of the abandoned reception building's rear parking lot and then pulled me off. My terror then turned into a complete and debilitating paralysis as he dragged me deeper into the bushes and sexually assaulted me several times. My mind was reeling. I feared he was going to kill me. I imagined I was going to die an ugly and lonely death in the abandoned parking lot of a vacated wedding reception venue, a place where so many people once had celebrated the happiest day of their lives.

I was stunned that I was unable to move. I should have screamed or resisted the assault, and maybe I could have stopped it, but as it unfolded my body went completely limp. I was no warrior archangel Michael on this night. I had no power or will to do anything. No power to do anything, that is, but say a simple prayer, which is what I did.

As the sexual assault unfolded, the only reaction I mustered was instinctive and directed to the protector of the monastery, the woman I had seen so many mornings before on the monks' lovely stained glass window. I recited "The Hail Mary," a prayer most Catholics learn at a young age when they are taught to say the Rosary:

> Hail Mary, full of grace, the Lord is with thee.
> Blessed are thou among women,
> And blessed is the fruit of thy womb, Jesus.
> Holy Mary, Mother of God, pray for us sinners now,
> and at the hour of our death. Amen.

I said it over and over again, hoping it was not the hour of my death. I prayed in a loud enough whisper that my assailant must have heard me. The sacred words contrasted sharply with the agonizing thrashing occurring on the dirt within the overgrown brush.

Perhaps my prayer made a difference and was answered. Perhaps the rapist recognized the prayer and had second thoughts about his deed. Abruptly and almost miraculously, he broke off his assault, sternly warned me not to tell anyone what had happened and let me go. I felt very lucky. I pulled my pants up and ran to my bike. Tears stained my face as I raced back to our apartment. My mom and sister were home by then. As I stumbled through the door, they saw my underpants hanging off one of my shoes and asked, "What happened?" In a panicked voice, choking back sobs, I told them. Mom was shocked and outraged. She immediately called the police and an officer came to our apartment to hear and record the story. He then went to the site of the assault but came back later and told us there was no one in the vicinity.

I did not return to the baseball team afterwards. I never got to be in the all-star lineup. However, I did get a close look at the criminal justice system. A week or two after I told my story to the police officer, I talked to an investigator and a detective. The detective called later and asked me to return to the police station and participate in a suspect lineup, done through a one-way mirror. Five men stood on the other side of the mirror and were told to turn from side to side and speak a few words. As I watched and listened to them, even with a large police officer and Mom at my side, my legs were weak and I felt chilling waves of paralyzing fear wash over me again, the same feelings I had on the night of the assault. I tried, but I was not able to identify any of the suspects as the assailant. The police closed the case for lack of evidence. To this day, I do not know who assaulted me or what became of him.

For some time after these events, I dealt with the traumatic aftermath. It did not wreck my life nor render me unable to function, but I felt its impact for several years. Not knowing the name, face, or identity of my assailant was both liberating and incarcerating. He was no one and nowhere. He was everyone and everywhere. Surprisingly, even though I had done them many times before, I feared doing routine and ordinary things, such as walking or riding on public buses alone. I was convinced that I might once again meet the man who had attacked me.

I also had flashbacks, including one rather intense panic attack as friends and I were walking around the darkened campus of Weber State College, looking to meet our ride home after a college football game. I had been on the campus many times before, knew it well, and generally had felt comfortable in the setting, but not on this particular evening. Every corner we turned now seemed unfamiliar and threatening. I had this strange and irrational fear that each person we encountered meant me harm. My heart raced and my shirt was drenched with sweat, even though it was a chilly autumn night.

It may be more painful to see your children get hurt than to get hurt yourself. Mom was equally or more traumatized by the assault. She told someone she blamed herself and the divorce, and at least by implication, my absent father, for what had happened. She also blamed the divorce for where we lived, so close to the site of the assault. She once angrily said that if she was not forced to work so many hours and, in the evening, she could have picked me up from baseball practice on the night in question, thus saving me from the fateful bike trip home.

Although traumatized, Mom also was extremely supportive. She told me repeatedly that it was not my fault and confidently encouraged me to get on with the wonderful future she said awaited me. She stood steadily by my side during the many police visits and medical appointments that followed, helping me deal with the dubious honor of being the first member of the family tested for a sexually transmitted disease. Thankfully, the test was negative. Mom also knew I was afraid to ride the public buses to school after the assault, and yet she helped me face my fears and continue to ride them anyway. I never caught her in the act, but I am fairly certain she discreetly, and from a distance, followed me to the bus stop more than once to make sure I had made it aboard without incident.

She also said I should talk with an adult male about what happened. For this task, not surprisingly, she chose two priests. One of them was Father Manny, the abbot of the monastery. I did not understand why I had to talk to anyone, and never told many people about what had happened, but I trusted her and so I took her advice. The conversations were awkward at first, but Mom must have briefed them in advance about what had occurred, because they both said tremendously reassuring and comforting things.

At the appointed hour when I was to meet with Father Manny, I approached his office with trepidation. I had never been in there before, and he was a busy and important man. His office was on the southwestern side of the abbey, down the hall from the guest quarters and next to the office of my friend the gregarious Father Denis Murphy. I knocked on the door and heard a gentle knock in response, which I understood to be the traditional Trappist nonverbal method of telling a visiting knocker that it was acceptable to enter. I opened the door timidly. His wood-paneled office was small and simple but bathed in morning sunshine from several windows facing south and west. He smiled, stood, and welcomed me warmly.

After some small talk, I told him about the assault and that Mom had suggested I talk to someone about what had happened. He listened carefully and asked some questions to verify that I was not physically injured and to assess my state of mind about the incident. Then, without sharing any specific details, Father Manny told me that either a neighbor or stranger (I cannot recall which) had subjected him to something similar when he was a young man. Perhaps confirming the validity of the cliché that misery loves company, I was comforted knowing that he had endured and survived a similar trauma, only to become the strong leader and kind man he was on the day I talked with him.

The other priest Mom asked to speak with me was our family friend Father Fred Draeger. Before my family moved to Ogden, we went to Mass at St. Rose of Lima in Layton, Father Draeger's small church where my sister Moe got married. I suspect Father Draeger comforted and counseled Mom on several occasions after the divorce, and he also helped her later to obtain an annulment of her marriage. He was a Paulist priest from New Jersey who came to his vocation later in life, in his thirties, after serving in the Air Force and working several years as a wax engraver in New York City. The famous Catholic television star, New York Bishop Fulton J. Sheen, ordained him in 1953.

Father Draeger was a bespectacled, serious man, but he relaxed around us, especially when he came to dinner at our apartment several times. He seemed especially fond of Mom's delectable pork roast. During these frequent mealtime visits, he often would loosen the top of his black Roman collar shirt, which until then I had not realized was possible as either a matter of fashion or dogma. He usually also brought along his closest friend and much-loved companion, a brown-and-black dachshund named Bertha. Bertha liked Mom's pork roast too.

Just because the first therapeutic talk about the sexual assault went so well with Father Manny does not mean I was eager to repeat the process with Father Draeger. Perhaps he sensed my anxiety, for he suggested we meet at my home. We sat together in our small apartment living room. It was bathed in various shades of gold, red, brown, and green, reflecting Mom's love for the colors of early autumn. Despite the warm environment and the friendly, polite preliminary chatter, my stress must have been obvious—as we met, my right leg bounced, in rapid-fire machine gun-like fashion.

Finally, I gripped and steadied my right leg, took a deep breath, and blurted out what had happened. Father Draeger and I discussed how the assault was bad enough, but how I also felt added shame and embarrassment because I was a male who had been unable to defend myself against a sexual assault by another male. He discounted the notion that I should have defended myself like the warrior archangel after whom I am named. He told me that my feelings were perfectly normal, but that I had done nothing wrong and had nothing to feel ashamed about. He said the fault was with the attacker, and that I needed to work diligently to not let what had happened define me either now or in the future. His words helped me understand that while the assault had happened to me, and was something I could never change, it was only one of many things— some good but some bad—that would happen over a lifetime and which, along with my reactions to such events, would sculpt me into the "fine man" I would soon become.

In hindsight, there was no need to be so nervous when I met with Father Draeger. He was a man of great compassion. At his funeral Mass about five years later, the Utah bishop described Father Draeger's devotion to his flock, noting, "Nothing was too much trouble for him in ministering to their spiritual needs, and, often to their material needs. When people came to him with their difficulties, which was quite frequently, he was a patient listener and a wise counselor."[2] His Utah friend Monsignor William H. McDougall echoed the sentiment, explaining, "People continually sought him out at the center because he was always available, always had time—or made time—for people. Personally, I think that is about the toughest job in the priesthood—to be always available. It is like being picked to death by butterflies."[3]

Father Draeger helped again a few years later. As I was getting ready for college, he gave me a check for $1,000, what he called a "scholarship." He repeated the gift the next year. He said he had some extra pension or retirement funds he wanted to put to good use. I really needed the financial help. My chosen college, the University of Notre Dame, was expensive to attend, and I was cobbling together all the financial resources possible to cover the costs. I found out fifteen years later, from my father's sister Florence O'Brien Niewenhous, that the "scholarship" money actually had come from my father. He suspected that I would not have accepted the assistance if he had offered it to me directly, so he convinced Father Draeger to serve as the conduit.

Father Draeger's little white lies helped two people with one gesture. He knew I needed the financial help, and his little trick helped me get it notwithstanding my relationship with my father, which was strained at best and could be more accurately described as nonexistent. Father Draeger also helped my father do something kind, and helped me appreciate my father, at least posthumously, for this kind act. Like my other pastor Father John LaBranche, we lost Father Draeger too soon. He passed away in 1981, at age 69, after complications related to heart surgery. The Salt Lake City church where his funeral was held a few days later overflowed with the hundreds of people whose lives he had touched.

Other than Father Manny and Father Dreager, I never told any of the monks, priests, or nuns I knew about the sexual assault, but I suspect Mom did. It makes sense that she talked with some of them about the feelings she had, perhaps unfairly blaming herself for it. I did not notice it then but looking back I now realize they all were more protective of me. It almost was as if I had my own network of living and breathing guardian angels watching over me, connecting me quite personally to the words of Psalm 91:11–12: "For he will give his angels charge of you to guard you in all your ways. On their hands they will bear you up, lest you dash your foot against a stone."

Many years later, grown and now with my own family, I toured the Vatican Museums in Rome and saw many splendid and historic tapestries displayed in a long hallway that leads into the Sistine Chapel. After enjoying the tapestries, and while standing for just a few moments and staring upward at the glorious Michelangelo paintings on the Sistine Chapel ceiling and walls, I realized that the story of the Catholic Church's interaction with its children during the last half of the twentieth century is a new large, intricate, and complicated tapestry that the Church also now owns and that is on display for all the public to see. The acts of child abuse reflected on this tapestry were terrible crimes and should have been handled like any other criminal behavior. The abuse and subsequent cover-up also were sins, a betrayal of trust, and a breach of promises of devotion made by the abusing priests. The involved priests and bishops failed the test of the Good Shepherd. They did not care for the flock as would Jesus. They let wolves attack lambs.

Yet, the far too many incidents of abuse and cover-up represent only some, and not all, of the many fibers in the fabric of this new tapestry. The threads of stories like my own also are woven into the cloth of this history. I was a victim of sexual assault, too, but it came from without, not from within, the Church. And it was the devotion of my mother, and of Catholic priests and monks, that rescued me from it.

The tremors and aftershocks of the child abuse scandal shook my faith and trust in the Church down to their core foundations, leaving me with debris and rubble to sift through. I did not want nor enjoy such an unpleasant experience, but it was an unexpected gift. Because of the crisis, I saw with clear eyes those revealed foundations again, for the first time in a long time. I am trying to rebuild my house of faith and trust on that bedrock. And someday, on renovated and refurbished walls, I hope to hang my own sad but lovely version of this tapestry.

■ ■ ■

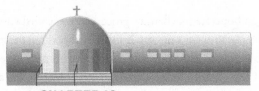

CHAPTER 16

A Saint among the Saints

Tʜᴇ ᴡᴏʀᴅs "Cᴀᴛʜᴏʟɪᴄ sᴀɪɴᴛ" ᴀɴᴅ "Uᴛᴀʜ" ʀᴀʀᴇʟʏ ᴀʀᴇ ᴜsᴇᴅ together in the same sentence. Yet, the Utah home of the Latter-day Saints has a wonderful, if little known, connection to one of the newest of the Catholic saints, Mother Teresa of Calcutta. She visited Utah in 1972, staying at Holy Trinity Abbey in Huntsville. I was there.

A few weeks before the highly anticipated visit, some excited monks told us the sensational news that someone they called an amazing person, and perhaps a living saint, was coming to the abbey in October. Sure, we all know the name now—Nobel Peace Prize winner in 1979, given a state funeral to rival that of Princess Diana during the year they both died in 1997, beatified by Pope John Paul II in 2003, and then canonized a saint by Pope Francis in 2016. In awarding Mother Teresa the Nobel Prize, the Norwegian Nobel Committee stated, "The loneliest, the most wretched and the dying have, at her hands, received compassion without condescension, based on reverence for man."[1] Fewer people knew of her in 1972, including us, but the Huntsville Trappists knew all about her. To them, she was a Catholic rock star, and they were some of her biggest fans.

After we got the news of her visit, I learned about her good works helping the poor, homeless, dying, and unwanted in the streets of Calcutta, India, and other large cities. One of the Holy Trinity monks, Brother Nicholas, had worked with her in Calcutta and they were close friends. Mother Teresa relied on him to screen men who wanted to join her order in the United States. Brother Nicholas was a big, strong man. He hailed from Grand Junction, Colorado, from a wealthy family that had formed and operated a chain of grocery stores called City Market, later owned by the Kroger Company. Brother Nicholas ran the monastery farm, doing a lot of the labor-intensive farm work himself. He eventually returned to Utah from India, overcome at times by malaria as well as by the difficult and daunting problems confronting Mother Teresa. She came to Utah to see him.

The book and a related movie called *Something Beautiful for God*, produced by the English writer Malcolm Muggeridge, tell her story well. I have an old and tattered 1971 version of the book that Mom acquired during our monastery days. The book and movie both draw their name from a comment in a letter that Mother Teresa wrote to Muggeridge when she agreed to work with him on these projects. She told him, "Now let us do something beautiful for God."[2] It was a phrase she used frequently to describe her work, and it aptly summed up her motivations and desires.

She was born of Albanian parents in Skopje, Yugoslavia. Her Albanian name, Anjeze Gonxhe Bojaxhiu, means something like "rosebud" or "little flower." As a young woman, Mother Teresa joined an order of Irish nuns, worked and studied in Ireland, and eventually in 1946 lived, taught, and worked at the Loreto convent school in Calcutta. While she was teaching, the great poverty outside the gates, in the city around her outside the school's enclave, distressed her. Soon, she received permission to live and work in the city's slums instead. Her work started modestly: "At first I had only five rupees, but gradually, as people came to know what I was doing, they brought things and money."[3] She formally started her order, the Missionaries of Charity, in 1948. The Utah monastery was getting started at about the same time.

As her Utah visit drew near, the monks gave us more details about her itinerary. She would be attending an early morning Mass at the abbey, staying for a short visit, spending time with her friend Brother Nicholas, addressing the monks, and meeting with some of her American volunteer coworkers. The monks relaxed their rules prohibiting women in their cloistered areas so that Mother Teresa could speak to them in their chapter room, a large meeting room near the church. (So far as I know, she is the only woman given that honor.) They told us the exact date of the visit, and what time to arrive, to possibly meet her. It felt like insider information.

On the day of the visit, October 19, 1972, we got to the monastery early for the 6:20 a.m. Mass. Father Manny, Brother Nicholas, and others had picked Mother Teresa up the evening before at the Salt Lake City International Airport. Father Manny later recalled that no one at the airport noticed them or her, in part because a large crowd there waited to see the Osmond family.[4] The Osmonds, a group of talented and clean-cut boys all from the same Utah Latter-day Saint family, had reached the top of the charts just the year before with their hit song "One Bad Apple." Just a few years later, a variety show featuring Donny Osmond and his sister Marie also would reach record audiences.

Before Mass on the day of Mother Teresa's visit, we waited with about a dozen other insiders for her to arrive at the church. At that time, the chapel had a visitors' section in the back, with wooden pews downstairs and also in the balcony. We sat upstairs, in the second row, and fortuitously just behind Mother Teresa. She arrived wearing a black sweater, her simple white sari robe with the blue trim, and sandals with socks. As I watched her from behind during the first part of Mass, I noticed how tiny she was. At my young age, I was already taller than she was. Her face was worn, homely, and wrinkled, her nose was bulbous, and you could not see any of her hair. Still, even I could detect that she radiated with an intense inner beauty.

The monks all gathered around the altar during the part of the Mass known as the Liturgy of the Eucharist. This was after the Bible and Gospel readings, and during the Offertory and the Consecration of the bread and wine on the altar. As a male, I was welcome to join the monks around the altar along with other men. I always was the youngest person there. I felt honored and self-conscious at the same time. I remember a very serious-looking monk, Father David Kinney, intensely staring at me on many occasions but smiling eventually. I gloated to Mom and my sister Karen about this special status afforded to me, gently taunting them because the women had to stay in the back of the church.

On the day of Mother Teresa's visit, however, they turned the gloating tables around on me. There is one part of the Mass, called the Sign of Peace, where the congregants greet each other, shake hands, and wish each other peace. I was up at the altar for this part of the Mass, shaking hands with the monks, but my mother and sister were in the back of the church, right behind Mother Teresa. She turned around, shook both their hands, and warmly wished them well. My sister Karen later pointed out, several times, how I did not get to shake the living saint's hand as she did. I must admit, I was—and still am—jealous. The Mass ended, and we left, but Mother Teresa spent the day with the monks and met with her coworkers.

We took some wonderful photos of her, with Brother Nicholas towering by her side, walking up the sidewalk after Mass past us into the main entrance of the monastery. Father Manny walked just behind, along with another woman who had accompanied Mother Teresa on the trip. We also have a photo of Mother Teresa standing alone in the parking area with a gentle smile on her face, apparently patiently and kindly waiting as we took her picture.

During her visit, Mother Teresa had a number of meetings with her American coworkers and with the monks. One of her friends, Eileen Egan, a New York Catholic writer and activist, accompanied her on the trip and arranged to tape record some of the meetings at the monastery. The tapes are available for public review, along with various other historical materials about Mother Teresa that Egan produced or collected and eventually donated to the archives of the Catholic University of America.[5] Several years after the 1972 visit, I listened to the tapes and learned about her discussions with the monks.

As might be expected, Mother Teresa's Huntsville meetings and discussions covered many normal and somewhat mundane topics related to the details of running a charitable organization in the United States. These topics included legal issues, where to possibly locate missionary houses in America, whether to charge recipients for materials or viewing films or receiving newsletters (Mother Teresa gently but adamantly opposed charging anyone for anything), coordinating work with dioceses and existing groups (on this point, Mother Teresa said, "I would not like for anybody or any of those organizations to think that we are making something new . . . we don't want to break or destroy anything, but we must complete."), how and where to conduct coworker meetings, publicizing the work, the challenges in safely sending money to India, how to send receipts for various financial contributions (Mother Teresa instructed they must always "respect the mind of the donor"), and how and where people could volunteer to help.

The Huntsville tapes also provide some fascinating insights, in Mother Teresa's own words, into the essential nature of her service to the poorest of the poor or, as she called it, "the work." She emphasized a half dozen major themes and principles during her talks. First, she said the work of caring for the poor must be centered in Jesus Christ. Second, people should look first to help the poor in their own neighborhoods before seeking to help the poor in far-flung places. Third, the work can and should begin in a small way, by doing even just the "one thing" that may lead to more meaningful things. Fourth, volunteers should thank those who help them. Fifth, every person of any means can share in the work. And finally, although she and others chose to be poor to understand the poor, those doing the work must do it with joy and a smile. Catholic saints do not publicly speak in Utah often, so her message not only is important, but also is historic.

On November 11, 1972, about a month after we saw Mother Teresa at the monastery, the *Ogden Standard-Examiner* carried a short article about the visit in the back of the paper, on the church pages. I remember no other news coverage. Knowing what we now know, the only published article seems to downplay and understate the occasion, saying in part:

> A Catholic nun who has gained recognition for universal work with the poor has counseled 16 of her American coworkers at a retreat in the Monastery of the Holy Trinity here. Mother Teresa of Calcutta said missionary workers must pattern their lives after the manner of the Missionaries of Charity, a congregation of Catholic sisters she founded in 1950.[6]

The monks were way ahead of the news cycle on this one. They knew what an important visit it was, and what an important visitor she was, and they knew that Mother Teresa was a person who would soon become much better known worldwide.

But who was she really? As happens to any public figure, some have criticized her motives, methods, manners, or beliefs. Still, how can one not admire someone who with no thought of personal gain, routinely picked up abandoned, unwanted, and dying strangers from the street and compassionately cared for them during their last days of life? Malcolm

Muggeridge's 1971 book and film said time would "decide whether she is a saint. I only say of her that in a dark time she is a burning and shining light; in a cruel time, a living embodiment of Christ's Gospel of love."[7] Posterity (and Pope Francis) made the decision, and she was canonized Saint Teresa of Kolkata in September 2016, almost forty-five years after I met her. Or, as my dear sister Karen would say, after I almost met her.

Because I knew the Utah monks, I had a living and breathing education about the virtues of simplicity and compassion. Seeing a living and breathing Mother Teresa, even for just a few moments, and learning her story, was the advanced course, the capstone, in that education. I have seen people who are saintly, including many of the monks and their neighbors. Mother Teresa is the only such person I have seen who holds the official title . . . for me, the saint among the saints.[8]

■ ■ ■

CHAPTER 17

College and Vocation

D URING HIGH SCHOOL, I STILL VISITED THE MONASTERY, BUT SPENT
less time there. I was busy, suffering from the common Catholic malady
of not knowing how to say no. I worked on many school activities
such as debate, drama, newspaper editor, yearbook staff, and student
council, and, of course, schoolwork also demanded a lot of my time.
As a typical self-conscious, self-obsessed, and foolish teenager, I also
was hypersensitive about the company I kept. I was not sure it was cool
visiting the monastery a lot. I was a believing and practicing Catholic, but
I did not want peers to label me as some kind of a religious fanatic.

High school was an intense and perplexing four years of trying to
figure out who I was, physically, emotionally, intellectually, spiritually,
sexually. At least I was able to enjoy and endure it with good company
and an interesting cast of characters, including the thirty-five members
of the Class of 1979. My friend John Zeuthen—perhaps the wittiest
person I ever met—taught me all about *Monty Python's Flying Circus*
and never failed to make me laugh. My academic rival (and later
roommate and best man) Marc Dominquez reminded me that good
men can grow up without a father. Defying the gender stereotypes of
the time, classmate Elizabeth Buller consistently edged me out in the
competition for top of the class awards in math. Shawn Alfonsi, whose
Italian father had been an American POW in Utah, was so kind that
he once wrecked his car trying to give me a ride home on a snowy day.
My elementary school girlfriend Jill Pauli blossomed into a smart and
beautiful young woman in high school, making me regret that I once
made her cry in third grade. And my Irish American colleagues Tim

Kenny and Laurie Sullivan taught me what they knew about Irish family culture, about which I was oblivious.

Our small St. Joseph's Catholic high school, with fewer than 150 students, had opened in 1954. Along with several Jesuit priests, the local Holy Cross sisters taught and worked at the school for several years. One was my good friend and the school principal, Sister Patricia Ann Thompson. She took her final vows as a Holy Cross sister in 1948, earned a master's degree from Stanford University, and had many years of experience as a teacher and school administrator. Sister Patricia Ann probably had some challenging moments working with us high schoolers. Many of my schoolmates unfairly disliked her, probably because she enforced the rules on rebellious and immature teens. They created a derogatory nickname based on the initials of her full title and name—"SPAT"—and referred to her that way. What I saw, instead, was a deeply compassionate and caring woman.

Once, she hired me over the summer to care for the school lawns. It was a generous but foolish attempt to help our family financially. I was horrible at it. Over just a few days, I blew the gasket (not even sure what it is but I broke it) on one mower, caused damage to the blade of a riding mower, and took out a half a dozen or so sprinkler heads in the process. It would have been difficult to cause more damage intentionally. After all that chaos, the grass did not even look good. Sister Patricia Ann called me in and started to explain the problem in gentle terms. I already knew, and asked her to use my unpaid wages to cover the costs of the mayhem. She happily accepted the offer. This was my first negotiated settlement agreement, and I think I probably got the better end of the deal.

On another occasion, my father showed up at the high school in the middle of the day, unexpected, unannounced, and unwelcome. He said he wanted to see me. Sister Patricia Ann respected me enough to pull me out of class, talk to me first, and ask what I wanted to do. I was embarrassed to be pulled out of class and shocked that he would just show up out of the blue, given that we had had so little contact before that time. I asked her if I could decline his visit, and she said I could, and so I did. He did not press the issue and left. Perhaps he was just following the advice of his mother. In a letter, right after the divorce, she wrote, "Stay as close to the children as possible and in time you will be able to overcome any bitterness that might exist." I regret that I probably hurt his feelings by not agreeing to his impromptu visit, but I always will be grateful to Sister Patricia Ann. Even though my father was not threatening in any way, she made me feel safe, protected, and in control, and ensured me that my feelings in the matter were her top concern.

One sad morning in January 1977, we came to school to learn that a tragedy had unfolded on the school's parking lot the night before. A family friend and the father of several students, one from my own class, had been trying to get his daughter's broken-down car to run, and had jacked it up to work underneath. The jack slipped and the car fell. It crushed and killed him. The scene was horrific. Some of his children witnessed the accident and there was a lot of blood. Sister Patricia Ann had to manage the scene and its aftermath, comfort the family, deal with the authorities, and, when everyone had gone, clean up the mess. She later let her guard down and told me that the whole matter had been extremely difficult to endure. Yet, she answered this call to duty with grace, compassion, and dignity.

In 1977, after my sophomore year of high school, Sister Patricia Ann and her fellow Holy Cross sisters were called away to other service, a transfer resulting in part from a shortage of nuns within their order. Due to the loss of cheap nun labor and increasing costs of operating schools, the Catholic Diocese of Salt Lake City strongly considered closing the school, unable and unwilling to underwrite its operations. Led by a devoted alum, teacher, and coach named Paul Willard, however, parents and friends of the community rallied and raised enough money to keep the school going for a few more years. The generous family of my classmate, Patty Evans, contributed mightily to this financial effort then, and for many decades afterwards. Tuition was $750 per year, about one-fifteenth of the comparable Catholic school tuition I paid for my kids some forty years later. I still have no idea how my mother paid even the relatively modest tuition costs of many years ago, but my guess is that the school helped her significantly with subsidized tuition. In other words, we got a lot of help from a wider, caring community.[1]

I worked hard and did well in high school, despite a senior year scandal when I got in serious trouble (rightfully so) for drinking beer with classmates after winning the statewide championship in a debate event. I wanted to attend college out of state, ideally at the University of Notre Dame in South Bend, Indiana. It was a big reach for a poor kid from a small town. I took the required tests, did well, and prepared the relevant application papers. The application form asked about my father. My response was painfully blunt. I wrote about the divorce and how I had no knowledge of his whereabouts. Asked to write a self-evaluation letter describing my strengths and weaknesses, I mentioned that I was a good student, occasionally lazy, but working on this weakness because I did not want to waste my talents. I explained that spiritually, I felt the "Blessed Trinity watches over our lives and guides us." Maybe, subconsciously at least, I was thinking about the Abbey of the Holy Trinity. I identified my greatest strength as being the love and support of my mother. I told Notre Dame I had room to grow and mature, but thought I had the right stuff to thrive at the university.

Father Manny offered to help with the application process and wrote one of my required letters of recommendation. His January 11, 1979, letter explained that my mother, sister, and I had "been coming to [the] Abbey regularly for the Sunday and holy day Eucharists" and for other prayer services such as Compline. As a result, he told Notre Dame, we were, "well known to many of [the] monks." He noted that, "because Mike's father apparently deserted his mother many years ago, Mike has looked to us for guidance." He kindly described me as "not spoiled," as "reasonably mature for his age," and as "religious without being fanatical." His letter ends with a specific and interesting Utah reference: "Since there is a very strong Mormon community in Utah, and since Catholics represent only five percent of the total population, I think that it is important that we have well educated Catholic laymen in the state who can be representative of the Church in whatever professional field they enter."

I suppose that my college application stood out a bit, coming from a non-Catholic place like Utah and including a recommendation letter from the Trappist abbot who lived there. Father Manny also was generous enough to ask the family of Brother Nicholas to put in a good word for me. His family, the Prinsters, owned the City Market grocery chain, and several of Brother Nick's nieces and nephews had attended Notre Dame. Thanks—once again—to a lot of help from a lot of people, on February

9, 1979, I was accepted into Notre Dame, and later obtained enough financial aid (and low-interest loans) to try to make it work for four years.

In August 1979, Mom took me to the Salt Lake City International Airport to catch an airplane flight to Chicago, and then on to South Bend, to launch my college career. Until our trip to the airport, I had not fully contemplated how my decision about where I would attend college would change her life. She grabbed me and gave me a tear-filled hug and turned to leave as I walked to the plane. It was a bittersweet departure, and I had a twisting, empty, and slightly nauseated feeling in my stomach as I boarded the plane.

College was a great experience, but my college classmates did not know exactly what to make of me. Most of them hated disco music, which still was popular at my Utah high school. Their jeans were straight-legged at the bottom, mine were flared. Most of them had never met anyone from Utah. I was asked the same three basic questions over and over again. "Are you Mormon?" "Do you know Donny and Marie?" "Can you really float in the Great Salt Lake?" My answers, of course, were "no," "no," and "yes, but the millions of brine flies will annoy the heck out of you!"

I also had some interesting misadventures getting there and back from college. The first year, I had the rare luxury of flying to college, but rising airfares soon challenged my travel budget. For my sophomore year, I retraced part of the Utah monks' 1947 train trip, only in the opposite direction and over three decades later. I hopped on Amtrak. The rail-side mountain scenery was amazing, starting in Utah and continuing through Colorado, where the tracks teeter on some spectacular cliffs and cross over the Continental Divide. I spent a hot and sleepless night in Nebraska when we lost air-conditioning in our train car. Nebraska is a long state, and it was a long night, too dark even to watch the corn grow. It was breathtaking, however, the next morning to cross and to see, for the first time, the mighty and muddy Mississippi River, the border between Iowa and Illinois. The rail journey climaxed with a few glimpses of the towering high rises around Chicago's Loop.

One of the journeys home from Indiana after the school year ended was memorable, too, not because of my encounter with scenery, but because of my encounter with Colorado police. Some college classmates were traveling west after school had ended, using something called the

"Driveaway" car-shipping program. This program brought together students who needed wheels with a car that needed to be transported across the country. We were driving a large car, either a Buick or a Cadillac, to an auto dealership near Denver. My plan, at the end of the drive, was to visit my Uncle Jack, Mom's brother, who had a clothing store in Denver, and then catch a cheap flight home to Utah. I ended up with the assignment to deliver the car to the dealership because the other student passengers had final destinations along the way and short of Denver.

It was about a sixteen-hour drive, and we took turns and drove straight through the night. I finished the last leg alone early in the morning, arriving in Denver way too early to deliver the car because the dealership did not open until about 10 a.m. Tired from the trip, I parked in a strip mall nearby and promptly fell asleep on the front seat of the car. I woke up to the noise of a local police officer tapping on the window. I probably looked disheveled after the long drive and the short nap. In a stern voice, he announced, "I need some identification, and what are you doing here?" As I explained the situation, I noticed that his partner had suddenly appeared at the car's passenger side window. I had not done anything wrong, but was apprehensive, and so I was nervously tapping my hands on the seat between my legs. The officer looked down and suddenly shouted, "Get your hands on the top of the steering wheel, now!" His partner immediately put his hand on his gun but did not draw it. "Get out of the car now," said the officer. I calmly complied, despite feeling sick and freaked out.

Once I was out of the car, the officer patted around the area below the driver's seat and I realized that he thought I was reaching for a weapon. We both were relieved that he did not find anything there. I handed him the car's registration papers, which explained the drive-away program. My name was not on the papers because I had not set it up, so I spent about fifteen minutes explaining, three or four times, how another person had made the car arrangements and how I had dropped her off earlier on the trip. The officer stared at me and barked, "Can I search your car?" Resisting my prelaw (today, I'm a lawyer) urges to argue the point, I consented because I knew I had nothing to hide and I wanted the ordeal to end. They went through the front and back seats and the trunk. As they did, I suddenly had a rather intense fear that perhaps, unbeknownst to me, one of my fellow student travelers, none of whom I knew very well, might have transported some contraband. Luckily, none of them had. After the search yielded nothing of concern apart from a smelly bag of dirty laundry, the officers let me go. No longer sleepy and with adrenalin coursing through my body, I delivered the car to the auto dealership, met my uncle for lunch, and got out of town as quickly as possible.

Like high school, college was a busy time. It also was eye-opening. I met a variety of people from all over the country. They talked, dressed, and seemed much different from me or the people I knew back home. One such fellow was a quiet guy who lived down the hall and around the corner. Several people in the dorm told me he was gay. Some shared it as a sort of neutral and nonjudgmental information point, but at least one or two people told me in a sneering, stigmatizing, homophobic way. I imagine it was not easy being gay in the late 1970s. I had not, at least as far as I knew at the time, met any gay guys. I talked to him once or twice, and he was nice and quiet and kept to himself. On occasion, he did have another male guest visit him in his room. One night, this private act caused a rather public scene.

Most people did not bother him, but another fellow in the dorm clearly did not like our gay dorm mate, apparently for no reason other than because he was gay. On the night in question, he slid a lighted firecracker under my neighbor's door and raced down the hall to escape. I was studying in my room with my door open, so I saw and heard this play out. Probably resigned to such harassment, my neighbor never opened his door or left his room. I did. As the other fellow was running away, I walked out my door, angrily blocked his way, and said, "Knock it off and leave him alone!" The surprised perpetrator said nothing in response, but he gave me an angry look and rolled his eyes at me. We did not have many friendly exchanges afterwards but near as I could tell, he left my neighbor alone the rest of that year. I was not trying to be a hero or activist or advocate in that moment. It just offended my sense of fair play that someone who was not bothering anyone should have to put up with firecrackers being hurled under the door of what, at that time, was his home.

Because I was so far away from Utah during four years of college, I did not see the Trappist monks often, but there were many other opportunities for spiritual edification. Notre Dame's campus features lovely twin lakes named after St. Mary and St. Joseph, as well as a replica of the Lourdes grotto, cave and all. The University's historic Sacred Heart Basilica, built in 1888, was home to the weekly Sunday high liturgy Mass affectionately known as "smells and bells" because of its use of handbells, incense, colorful vestments, a full choir, and other pageantry. I did not frequent smells and bells very often because late each Sunday night at 10:30 p.m., the men of our dormitory would gather in our chapel for Mass. It was a monastic-like moment, with almost a hundred tenor and baritone male voices singing songs such as Dan Schutte's "Glory and praise to our God." One college friend—John Fitzgerald—remarked that someday we would miss hearing those voices. He was right.

I also met several fine priests from the Congregation of the Holy Cross (CSC), the religious order that founded Notre Dame. Father Gene Gorski, a scholar in French and world religions, was the rector of our residence hall. He patiently mentored hundreds of young men through their sometimes-tumultuous college years and called us all "stalwarts" and "pillars." Late one night, I saw an office light burning under the Golden Dome in the window of the university president, Father Theodore M. Hesburgh. Following a well-established Notre Dame tradition, I found a way into the building and knocked on his door. The busy priest and civic leader took five or ten minutes to shake my hand, ask how school was going, and inquire how an O'Brien ended up in Utah. One autumn the campus minister, Father Bill Toohey, a 50-year-old former Marine, preached in our dorm chapel. He reminded us that we never know when we will need to do something to make a difference in the life of someone else, explaining, "Jesus always comes to see us at what seems like the wrong time." The exclamation point to his message arrived just a few weeks later, when Father Toohey contracted and died of viral encephalitis.

During these years I sent letters home to the monastery to update my status and tell them of my many adventures, one of which included seeing Pope John Paul II, along with about a million other people, when he visited Chicago in 1979 during my freshman year. I started to regularly hear back from Father Jerome Siler, one of the Utah monks I had not known well before. We became pen pals and soon, friends.

Father Jerome was another one of the original founders of the monastery. He was born in Philadelphia, served as an English Army chaplain during World War II, and lived and studied in Jerusalem, Egypt, and North Africa before coming to Utah. He was a scholar, and among other things, the abbey librarian.[2] He also belonged to the national Mariological Society of America, which according to its bylaws is "a Catholic theological association dedicated to studying and making known the role of the Blessed Virgin Mary in the mystery of Christ and the Church and in the history of salvation."[3] Born in 1901, Father Jerome was in his late seventies when I first met him. His vision was failing. Mom had tended to him at St. Benedict's Hospital after he had cataract surgery on both of his eyes. She brought him ice cream as he was recovering from the surgery and they became friends. He would call her at home from time to time just to check on her. Because of his eye problems, he wore thick glasses and often walked in a bashful, tentative, and uncertain manner that reminded me of the cartoon character Mr. Magoo.

I saved the letter he sent to me just before I graduated college. It is addressed, "Dear Michael, Dear Friend." His letter thanked me for "including your Holy Trinity Brothers in your mailing list," and sweetly said, "I would do anything to be present to see you arrayed in scholastic attire on that long-looked for day of graduation." After telling me he would keep me in mind on graduation day, he conveyed that all was well at the abbey. Demonstrating the utterly charming simplicity of a monk, he also reported excitedly: "[Our] real good news is our lilac is now full of buds." He wrote that he was eagerly anticipating singing the Paschal Alleluias at Easter. His letter closed with this note: "Your good Mother promised to bring you out here when you appear anew in Utah—another glad day for us."

Father Jerome was appropriately excited for the Paschal celebration. Each spring at the monastery came the highpoint of the Christian liturgical year—and of a monk's year—Easter. Watching their liturgical celebrations, I appreciated the Easter story as a wonderful, three-act, dramatic play or, as we Catholics call it, the Easter Triduum, or "three days." Palm Sunday, the celebration of Jesus's entry into Jerusalem, kicks things off the week before Easter. The Triduum, however, starts with Holy Thursday, the Mass of the Last Supper. During this celebration,

Father Manny would wash the bare feet of twelve of his brother monks, just as Jesus did. The next day, he would lead the monks in the liturgy commemorating the crucifixion, Good Friday, and the veneration of a large wooden cross.

Finally, much the same as they did at Christmastime, at Easter the monks joyfully participated in a wonderful vigil service held at midnight on Holy Saturday and continuing on through early Easter Sunday morning. In the back of the abbey chapel, or outside just in front of it, in near-total darkness, the monks would consecrate the Easter candle, light it, and share its light with all in attendance, who, with their own individual candles, would eventually illuminate the entire church building. Then, with bells ringing, the regular Mass would begin. Unlike the regular Mass, however, there were nine readings proclaimed at the Easter Vigil—a scriptural marathon, what I considered a liturgical rendition of the Bible's greatest hits.

It started with Genesis 1:3 and the creation story: "And God said, 'Let there be light,' and there was light." In the next reading from Genesis 22:17, God blessed Abraham for his obedience: "I will indeed bless you, and I will multiply your descendants as the stars of heaven and the sand which is on the seashore." Moses followed, leading the Israelites out of captivity in Egypt in Exodus 14:15–15:1. The Prophet Isaiah spoke up next, with tender and reassuring words of God's love (Isaiah 54:10), "For the mountains may depart and the hills be removed, but my steadfast love shall not depart from you and my covenant of peace shall not be removed." Sometimes, by the end of the fourth reading, I was getting a little sleepy, but I persevered.

In the fifth reading, Isaiah issued an invitation for a closer relationship with God (Isaiah 55:1): "Ho, everyone who thirsts, come to the waters." The prophetic scribe Baruch then reminded us that, "If you had walked in the way of God, you would be dwelling in peace for ever" (Baruch 3:13). Yet another prophet, Ezekiel, next told of the saving forgiveness of God: "A new heart I will give you, and a new spirit I will put within you; and I will take out of your flesh the heart of stone and give you a heart of flesh" (Ezekiel 36:26). Just before the Gospel, St. Paul's Letter to the Romans announced the great hope of resurrection for all of us, and explained, "We were buried therefore with him by baptism into death, so that as Christ was raised from the dead by the glory of the Father, we too might walk in newness of life" (Romans 6:4). Finally, the Liturgy of the Word reached its dramatic climax with the Gospel reading, when the angel at the tomb announced the resurrection of Jesus, saying, "He is not here; for he has risen, as he said" (Matthew 28:6).

After graduating from Notre Dame, and before starting law school at the University of Utah in the fall of 1983, I kept Mom's promise to Father Jerome and made an overnight retreat by myself at the abbey.

It was a wonderful reunion with my old friends. I did not know then, but it also was a goodbye of sorts, as it was the last time I was able to spend a significant and uninterrupted amount of time at the monastery before law school, career, marriage, and fatherhood occupied so much of my time. By now, Father Manny had retired from his position as abbot and served as guest master. Of course, I met up with Father Patrick and Brother Boniface. I also walked over to the cemetery and paid my respects to my departed friends Father Denis and Willie Arrow himself, Brother Ferdinand. Yet, it was my visits with Father Jerome and Brother Lawrence (now known as David) Baumbach that were particularly memorable.

Brother Lawrence and I took a long walk together down Abbey Road. He was trying to increase vocations for the monastery, which always could use new recruits to the Trappist life. Without pressing, he asked me about my plans. I had considered joining Holy Trinity Abbey. The monks I knew all were good men, and I was attracted to the idea of trying to emulate them. Certainly, the notion that there is someone devoted to praying 24/7 for the betterment of the world is a comforting thought. There was a certain appeal to engaging in such a noble and necessary profession in such a spectacularly beautiful place, and the monastery already felt like home.

Yet, while I am at times a contemplative person, I doubted I could be one around the clock. Moreover, a stronger part of me wanted to attend law school and consider becoming a father in the traditional sense, through marriage and raising a family. I must admit that the monastery's 3 a.m. wake-up call time was not a selling point either, especially for a night owl like me. I told Brother Lawrence how I felt. He listened carefully, and was supportive, but I also sensed disappointment from him when he heard my news. I took that as a compliment.

During my retreat visit with Father Jerome, we chatted about school and family. He insisted several times that while I was attending law school, I must contact the "OPs," and he told me that the "OPs" would take good care of me. I nodded politely, not knowing what he meant at first, but soon realized he was referring to the Dominican priests who operated the Newman Center at the University. Newman Centers are youth programs for college-age Catholics. In Salt Lake City, the Newman Center was its own parish, named in honor of St. Catherine of Siena, a fourteenth-century Dominican tertiary from Italy who cared for the sick and poor and worked to reform the Church. St. Dominic, the founder of the Dominican order, was a Spanish priest who lived in the early thirteenth century and dedicated his life to traveling and teaching and preaching the gospel. Like the OCSO (Order of Cistercians of the Strict Observance) that Trappists put at the end of their names, OP means "Order of Preachers" and is the designation the Dominicans use after their names. Father Jerome's counsel to connect with the OPs was one of the best pieces of advice I ever received.

I did connect with them, and it was at the Newman Center where I met my future wife, Vicki Comeau O'Brien. She was originally from Las Vegas and had come to the U of U on scholarship. About four years after we met, we got married at the Cathedral of the Madeleine in Salt Lake City, where a wonderful Dominican priest named Father Don Bramble—one of the best preachers I have ever heard—performed the ceremony. We have had a wonderful life together. I owe an eternal debt of gratitude to my monk matchmaker, Father Jerome.

In addition to meeting with Father Jerome during my post-college monastic retreat, I once again enjoyed the music of the abbey. Most young people love the popular music of their own generation and tolerate the music of their parents' generation. Not many of them, however, get to hear and learn Gregorian chants, the music of medieval monasteries. Because of the Utah monks, my personal life soundtrack came to include not just the music of the 1970s, but also the music of the 970s. I heard the Huntsville Trappists chant their daily Gregorian praises hundreds of times, most often at the services of Compline, Vespers, and None, but sometimes at Lauds and Sext too.

Each prayer service started the same basic way. The monks gathered in the simple church. Bells would peal from the chapel's bell tower, courtesy of the designated bell ringer. As the monks would bow, tenor and baritone voices would humbly implore, like clockwork, what is known as the doxology: "Oh God, come to my assistance. Oh, Lord, make haste to help me. Praise the Father, the Son and the Holy Spirit, both now and forever. The God who is and was and is to come, at the end of the ages." As the monks faced each other, one group looking north and the other south, the monastery cantor, Father Alan Hohl, played a note on his harmonica to get everyone on tune.

The abbey's Gregorian chants almost always were based on the Psalms—the Psalter—which the monks recited in its entirety every two weeks. For example, during my post-college retreat there, they chanted a version of the Fourth Psalm:

(North side)
When I call answer me oh God of justice.
From anguish you released me have mercy and hear me.

(South side)
Oh men how long will your hearts be closed?
Will you love what is futile and seek what is false?

It is the Lord who grants favors to those whom he loves.
The Lord hears me whenever I call him.

Fear him, do not sin, ponder on your bed and be still.
Make justice your sacrifice and trust in the Lord.

What can bring us happiness? Many say.
Lift up the light of your face on us oh Lord.

You have put into my heart a greater joy
Than they have from abundance of corn and new wine.

I will lie down in peace and sleep comes at once,
for you alone Lord make me dwell in safety.

(bowing)
> Praise the Father, the Son and the Holy Spirit,
> both now and forever.

The God who is and was and is to come,
at the end of the ages.[4]

The prayer service my family attended most frequently was Compline, a Trappist monk's end-of-the-day chant. It is a soothing liturgy, the monks' time to say goodnight to God. It typically opened with a comforting hymn such as this one:

> Oh God creator of all things, and ruler of the Universe, our days you clothe in radiant light, our nights you fold in peaceful sleep. Now that the day has run its course, and darkness covers things from sight, we beg for pardon, plead for grace, and ask protection for the night. Almighty Father hear our cry, through Jesus Christ our Lord most high, whom in the spirit we adore, who reigns with you forever more. Amen.

After chanting some psalms, the monks turned toward the altar, faced the beautiful Salve Regina window, and sang to Mary, their patroness, beseeching her to "intercede for us always to Jesus."

As the monks fell silent, their church bells rang out the Angelus, the call to prayer and goodwill commemorating the angel Gabriel's first greeting to Mary, the Mother of Jesus. The Utah bells clanged three chimes in three distinct sequences, and then rang constantly for a few moments as the monks left the church to retire for the night.

Compline was also the last service I attended during my Holy Trinity retreat in the summer of 1983. At the end, I walked as usual to the front of the church and joined the line of monks waiting for a blessing. Father Manny had blessed me there many times during the past decade. This time, I stood before the new abbot, Father Malachy Flaherty. He was a son of Kentucky farmers and Irish immigrants and was one of the pioneer Utah monks. He was known for having planted many of the trees on the monastery grounds, including his own small forest to the southeast of the place, designed to dry out a small marsh on the abbey's property. I bowed at the waist before Father Malachy and he smiled and doused me with holy water, a welcome traditional Trappist monk's blessing for the end of the day and for safety through the night.

A sprinkling of water is a form of baptism, which literally means bathing. I had been blessed this way often at the abbey, but now I was a college graduate and as tall, or taller, than most of the monks. I had a deep voice and facial hair—a red beard but no moustache, like Abraham Lincoln or a leprechaun. The blessing on this night seemed different and symbolically revealed what anyone already could see. The waters washed away the final traces of my boyhood and from them emerged a young man.

I left after Compline, at sunset, and began to drive home. Partway down the Abbey Road lined with some of Father Malachy's trees, I glanced up at the car's rear-view mirror. I could see where I was, was going, and had been—my past, my present, and my future—all just by looking at the mirror at that moment. I saw the connections between them and understood how one influenced the other. And I saw the receding reflected image of Abbey of the Holy Trinity, right next to my own reflection.

Thanks to my mother, I first came to the abbey in 1972 at age eleven, uncertain of whether I had a father. More than ten years later, I left the monastery as a grown man with at least a dozen of them. My past, my present, and my future were shaped, forever and for the better, by my decade as a boy monk. I drove home as night fell.

Darkness pervades all our lives. It often is an unwelcome companion, dreaded from the moment we glimpse one of its many garments, such as poverty, divorce, sexual abuse, and scandal, to name just a few. Thankfully, morning shadows night. Light stalks darkness, walks with us too, and enfolds us. For me, one of light's most recognizable garments is the simple black and white robe of a monk, and light's ever-soothing embrace is the sweet memory of my monastery mornings.

CHAPTER 18

A Boy Monk's Vows

D URING MANY YEARS OF CATHOLIC LIFE I LISTENED ROUTINELY while someone read the opening lines from the Gospel of John: "In the beginning was the Word, and the Word was with God, and the Word was God. . . . And the Word became flesh and dwelt among us."[1] These statements often perplexed me, but now I think I understand them better. The words express not only the central tenet of Catholicism and Christianity, but also the essential meaning of my friendship with the Utah monks.

John's words proclaim the doctrine of the Incarnation. Yes, this is theology, so perhaps your eyelids now are drooping just a bit. Stay with me . . . it is not that complicated and it actually is quite interesting. To incarnate means to embody in a human form. The Catholic Church catechism states, "The Son of God assumed a human nature to accomplish our salvation in it," emphasizing the divine role in this transaction, focusing on what a powerful God did to us and for us, a weak but beloved people. From this vantage point, the Incarnation occurs so God can save us, so that we can live and learn through God's Son, and so the sacrifice of Jesus on the cross will expiate and wash away our sins.[2] This theology centers on the undeniably wonderful things God has done for us: "For God so loved the world that he gave his only Son, that whoever believes in him shall not perish but have eternal life" (John 3:16).

This benevolent and powerful God the Father, the God on High, is the God featured in my favorite hymn from the Billy Graham crusades, "How Great Thou Art." For me, this awesome God the Father is a distant and unrecognizable figure, perhaps because I had no real relationship with my own father. Of course, I am not the first person to have faith that God exists, but also wonder exactly where God is. "I am told God lives in me," Mother Teresa wrote in a 1957 letter, "and yet the reality of darkness and coldness and emptiness is so great that nothing touches my soul."[3] Pope Francis described such uncertainty as normal, but explained "many doubts vanish because we feel the presence of God and the truth of the Gospel in the love that, by no merit of ours, lives in us and that we share with others."[4] In other words, because of the love we show each other, God is not so remote after all. This is the master key unlocking the mystery of the Incarnation.

Again, stay with me for just a little more theology. Catholic tradition explains that after the Incarnation, Jesus was not some kind of "a confused mixture," but rather remained fully human and fully divine at the same time. This means Jesus was a human being, like you and me, and that God became human. As my friend Father John LaBranche used to tell us in school, "Hey, Jesus had hair under his armpits!" So yes, the power of the awesome (but remote) God on high saves us through the Incarnation, but through the Incarnation we also give God a more recognizable shape and face, a less remote face, a human shape and face, and even armpit hair. Anyone who "fully accepts his or her own humanity and the humanity of others has at least implicitly accepted Christ, because Christ is in all of us and God is in Christ."[5] As Pope John Paul II said, "Jesus is the human face of God and the divine face of man."[6]

This is the sweet spot, the place where I find God and Jesus—in the faces, lives, and acts of love and kindness of other people. I am not a mystic, so without the Incarnation, I doubt I would have any kind of personal or meaningful understanding of God, let alone faith in God. Some may push back and say that I believe in people, not in God, but doesn't the Incarnation make them one in the same? As my monastery friend Father Patrick said to almost everyone he met: "When you walked through that door, Christ came into this room!"

Again, some fair pushback—this can be a precarious and perilous way to find God. Sometimes, looking into the face of another person reveals neither divinity nor humanity, but rather the stark absence of both. Imagine your image of God if you looked at another person, and returning your gaze was Adolph Hitler, Jeffrey Dahmer, Dylann Roof, or

a sexual predator? Yet, I believe there are far more good faces than evil
faces in the world, even if the evil ones capture most of the headlines.
Fortunately, with a few exceptions, these good faces have been the ones
looking back at me during my life. I have not always seen God in my
fellow humans, but I have often enough to believe this is the fundamental
way I encounter God.

Certainly, this was true during my encounters with my mother, the
monks, and many others you just read about. These encounters made
my life better. Time and again, my mother was there for me with love,
support, and wisdom, in one way or another, in both day-to-day life and
also in moments of turmoil or angst. She did all this in the midst of her
own serious personal crisis and pain. Our story could have had a much
different ending than it did. Instead, it is a story of how a devoted Irish-
Catholic mother helped a child of divorce become a man of faith, hope,
and love.

The monks made my life better too, in many of the same ways, but
more fundamentally because I saw them keep promises, by living vows
they made to God and to each other. The Trappist monks describe their
vows this way:

> A man or woman takes a vow because of the life-changing impact
> of a personal encounter with Jesus Christ and fascination with his
> way of being human. Far more than a legal obligation or social
> contract, religious vows are an expression that one is wholly
> given over to living the way Jesus lived: obediently, communally,
> chastely, and with great inward and outward simplicity. As Jesus
> himself was set on fire and ultimately consumed by his passion to
> do the Father's will, the Cistercian aspires to be a holocaust offered
> to God on the altar that is the monastic way of life.[7]

They take five solemn vows of "celibacy, of poverty, of obedience in
all things good, of stability (meaning that he remains a member of this
community), [and] conversion of manners (that is, to live the monastic
life to its fullest, without ever saying to himself that he has done enough)."[8]
Such promises, and the level of commitment necessary to keep them,
may sound irrelevant or foreign to most of us. Yet, even those who are

not monks will recognize and understand these values once they are translated from the monastic context.

The first of the five vows that Trappist monks take is the promise of obedience. In their clear and simple manner, they describe this vow as follows:

> As followers of Christ who came not to do his own will but the will of the Father Who sent him, Cistercians promise obedience to an abbot or abbess. Much more than the following of orders from a superior, our obedience is a quality of soul which makes us willing to put our own desires aside even to the point of preferring another's wishes.[9]

This description includes doing what the leader of the monastery asks you to do, but it also extends obedience beyond subservience and beyond the stereotype of the blind follower. Keeping such a promise involves a journey away from selfishness, a passage powered by the act of listening to others.

When mentioning obedience, the Bible often originally used the Greek word *hupakouo*, which means to listen, such as in the lovely image of listening for the knock at the door to find out who is there and to let them in.[10] It was such obedience, such listening, that brought the Trappists to Utah. It also was my own mother's "obedience," that is her "quality of soul" allowing her to focus on others, that brought my family and me to the Trappists. The remarkable capacity of the monks to put aside their own desires "even to the point of preferring another's wishes," is what transformed Holy Trinity Abbey from a dusty cattle ranch into such a special and sacred place. It is through the lens of this first Trappist vow that I first began to see and understand the awesome power unleashed when, in our own lives, we take the time to listen at the door for others.

Trappists also take a vow of stability. The essence of this second vow is a commitment to community. The Trappists explain this vow of stability as follows:

> By our vow of stability, we promise to commit ourselves for life to one community of brothers or sisters with whom we will work

out our salvation in faith, hope, and love. Resisting all temptation
to escape the truth about ourselves by restless movement from
one place to the next, we gradually entrust ourselves to God's
mercy experienced in the company of brothers or sisters who
know us and accept us as we are.[11]

People imagine monks as reclusive hermits, and see them as
hooded, distant, and lonely figures on a solitary search for God and
meaning. I did too. Yet, one of the Utah monks' cornerstone promises
actually propelled them into a life inextricably connected with others
with whom they could try to "work out" their salvation, "in faith,
hope, and love," all in an environment of accepting people "as we are."

Similarly, the lives of us non-monks are inextricably connected
to each other, to others who will love us and care for us, flaws and
all. Dorothy Day, the great Catholic advocate for the poor and for
workers, concludes her autobiography *The Long Loneliness* by writing,
"We have all known the long loneliness and we have learned that the
only solution is love and that love comes with community."[12] For a
boy like me, set adrift in the turbulent sea of divorce, to be accepted
and be part of a stable and functioning community of men such as
the monastery, even in an informal manner, was a gift and a lifeline.

Trappists also take a vow of poverty, which for them is a positive
state of mind and spirit, not just a matter of dollars and cents. They
explain their vow this way:

> To possess nothing of our own and to hold everything in
> common with our brothers or sisters is one means by which
> Cistercians seek to free themselves from the self-centeredness
> that separates us from God and others. Being poor with the
> poor Christ, we experience his need for God and God's manifest
> mercy who always shows compassion to those in distress.[13]

Those of us who do not live in a monastery likely will not live a
life of strict material poverty like the Utah monks. Yet, we all can try
to minimize the type of self-inflicted complexity that the American
cowboy poet and philosopher Will Rogers once described so well:

"Too many people spend money they haven't earned, to buy things they don't want, to impress people they don't like." On Facebook one day I read a post by the Dalai Lama recalling a saying in Tibetan that "at the door of the miserable rich man sleeps the contented beggar." He explained, "The point of this saying is not that poverty is a virtue, but that happiness does not come from wealth, but from setting limits to one's desires, and living within those limits with satisfaction."

The vow of poverty is a call for all of us to live with greater simplicity and increased compassion. In their daily struggle to "free themselves from the self-centeredness that separates us from God and others," the Utah monks did a lot of good for a lot of people. One of the best things they did was to provide a compelling model of how to live more simply and more compassionately. I saw this when I worked with Brother Boniface and when Father Patrick blessed me, and even when I chased a calf in a muddy field. I saw this when Mom, despite her own poverty, helped others in need. I saw this the day my family met—and I almost met—Mother Teresa when she visited the monastery.

The fourth vow that Trappists take is the promise of celibacy, which the monks have described as follows:

> Celibacy, the renunciation of married love, has as its aim to make the system free – to liberate the love of our hearts for service to the Lord Jesus and his church. This radical discipline, sustained only by prayer, does not separate us from the riches of human love, but is a means by which that love is taken up and fulfilled as a gift offered to the whole church in the world.[14]

Celibacy is a complex and mysterious promise, especially for us who choose the noncelibate life. It is not, as one might think, the simple question of whether or not to have sex. It actually means much more than just that in the monastic or religious context, where it is all about relationship. For example, to help my simple child's mind understand the concept, Mom always used to say that a priest or nun marries God, or Jesus. As writer F. Scott Fitzgerald keenly observed in *This Side of Paradise*, "Celibacy goes deeper than the flesh."

This vow also can be meaningful for those of us who are not celibate monks, for at the heart of celibacy is the notion of devotion. We love best and most enduringly when we love with devotion, whether to a partner in a noncelibate life, or to friends and family, or to the whole world in the celibate manner followed by my Trappist friends, by Father LaBranche, by Father Draeger, by my Jesuit teachers, and by the Holy Cross priests and sisters. Devotion makes these relationships work and grows their fruits.

The Trappists describe their fifth and final vow, called the conversion of manners, as follows:

Cistercians believe that people can change. Each of us takes a "vow of conversion" by which we promise to live the monastic way of life as a means of learning the truth about ourselves." Knowing ourselves as we really are, we become radically dependent upon the Lord Jesus who shows us God's mercy. Confident in God's forgiveness, we experience intimacy with God and are born to a new kind of life. Integral to the monastic way of life is the practice of voluntary poverty and celibate chastity.[15]

How might a non-monk apply such a concept to his or her own life? In *Apology*, Plato's account of the trial of Socrates, the Greek philosopher proclaims, "the unexamined life is not worth living." Several thousand years later, contemporary American writer Pat Conroy, in *My Reading Life*, said, "The writing of novels is one of the few ways I have found to approach the altar of God and Creation itself. You try to worship God by performing the singularly courageous and impossible favor of knowing yourself." Ultimately, my interactions with the Holy Trinity monks helped me to know myself better, to change, to mature, to grow into the imperfect but evolving person I am today, and to continue to grow into the better person I hope I will be tomorrow.

I never took the vows that the Trappists took, but their words and their actions imprinted upon me the true meaning of those promises. Years of watching the monks struggle to fulfill their promises to God and to others revealed, unexpectedly, the existence of a pathway for me, and indeed for all of us, to take as we search for a life filled with faith, hope, and love.

This path involves striving, like the monks, to keep five basic promises: (1) to listen and focus on others, (2) to build and sustain community, (3) to live with greater simplicity and more compassion, (4) to act with devotion in relationships, and (5) to develop self-understanding and try to grow from it, that is to change for the better.

The monks, priests, and sisters I knew taught me about fidelity, humility, mercy, forgiveness, kindness, perseverance, and hard work. They comforted us during difficult times, serving as unlikely, but reliable, sources of strength, encouragement, hope, and friendship. In them, I saw how to live below one's means, and do so contentedly, in the present moment. Watching them, I learned how to find joy in the smallest and simplest of the day's events, such as simple buds on a lilac bush. I learned to respect the sacred even while having a healthy sense of humor. I fear death less having watched them embrace it. I saw how happy someone can be without money, but also understood the value and happiness money can bestow when used in the right way, to help others. I witnessed firsthand the wide and ripple-like effect, around the world, of charity and small acts of kindness emanating from even a remote corner such as Huntsville, Utah.

I learned about human nature and humanity. The monks were men of God, but they also were just men. I saw them with awe, revered and admired them, but also appreciated them as fellow human beings. They were full of wit, humor, kindness, joy, sadness, courage, fear, flaws, perfections, imperfections, wisdom, confusion, answers, questions, compassion, uncertainty, grace, a thirst for peace and meaning, and, of course, love. They were different and set apart, yet they also were just like me. I have tried, with mixed success, to walk along the path they bequeathed to me, although I have done so with a different vocation. I may not have done it at all had I not met them . . . at the still point of my turning world.

I am not sure when I first heard it, but I also like another phrase coined by T. S. Eliot: "We shall not cease from exploration, and the end of all our exploring will be to arrive where we started and know the place for the first time."[16] My own exploration started in earnest when I saw a little girl hug our parish priest in the midst of the Church child-abuse scandal. I thought then of the words of the prophet Isaiah (11:6), "a little child shall lead them." When I saw that hug, despite my anger and disappointment at the people involved in the scandal, I knew that most children are not sexually abused by their priests. I knew that the overwhelming majority of priests are not sexual predators ready to pounce on the children placed in their trust. I also knew many Catholics like me had forgotten about, and desperately needed again to see, the loving and trustworthy face of their Church. I knew these Catholics were considering leaving the Church. Was I to join them?

In true lawyer-like fashion, I answered this question with another question: What is the Church? The Church is much like the Holy Trinity it reveres, three faces in one. It is an institution, a community of people, and a servant to those people. The institutional face of the Church is a "hierarchically structured, visible society which mediates salvation to its individual members through the preaching and teaching of the Word and the administration of the sacraments." The community face of the Church is "a people, whose principal task is the promotion and sustaining of personal growth through interpersonal relationships." The Church also is what the institution and people do, i.e., the visible face of a servant, "an agent of social change, whose task is the wise and courageous allocation of its own moral and material resources for the sake of the coming of the Kingdom of God among humankind—a kingdom of justice and peace as well as holiness and grace."[17]

I could easily leave behind the first face of the Church, the imperfect institution, where some bad shepherds committed abuse or covered it up. Less easily could I leave behind the other two faces of the Church, the community of the people of God or the servant seeking to bring about the kingdom of God on earth, a kingdom where no child is abused. Leaving the Church also would mean rejecting the spiritual and practical life legacy left to me by my friends the priests and nuns, by my Trappist brothers, and by my own mother. It would be heart-wrenching, to say the least, to divorce myself from a church that has produced such people, all of them in the mold of St. Francis of Assisi and St. Teresa of Calcutta.

And so, I persevere. I persist. I remain a Catholic today. I do so with less trust for institutional Church leaders. Once trust is breached, it takes time to restore it. I do so with more caution, trepidation, and doubt. Yet, I also do so with hope and optimism.

Many years ago, while studying theology at the University of Notre Dame, I took a one-year-long Catholic Church history course, covering 2,000 years in just two semesters. We studied the good and bad. This ranged from miracles to murders, from saints to sinners, charity to corruption, and inspirations to inquisitions. It was discouraging at times. Yet, despite all the turmoil caused by the imperfect humans running the Church, a basic perfect truth, a goodness, and a light survived. The essence of the Church's message prevailed during this tumultuous history, despite the best efforts of some to corrupt or destroy it.

That enduring essence is the Sermon on the Mount, proclaiming that blessed are the peacemakers, and the merciful, and those who hunger and thirst for justice. It is the soothing words of love and comfort found in the Twenty-Third Psalm. It is the Gospel words of Jesus commanding us to love one another and do unto others as we would have them do unto us. It is St. Paul reminding us in a letter that love is patient and kind, and endures all things, and that of the core virtues of faith, hope, and love, the greatest of these is love. The failure of too many to follow this very essential message caused the criminal child abuse and related scandal that now threatens the message itself. History confirms, however, that the Catholic Church is at its best, and overcomes its darkest hours, when it returns and remains firmly anchored to this core message of love.

When I arrived at the coincidental confluence of the awful child abuse scandal and the pending closure of my beloved Utah monastery, I was stuck there. I also knew, however, I could not linger between the scandalized church I had begun to hate and the church of my mother and the monks that I loved. At that moment, I did not know what I would choose to do, but at least I knew how to choose. I had to go backward in order to go forward. So, I did, and this book is the product of that journey into memory.

I have shared these stories because they are about love. The Catholic Church, those who care about it, and those abused by its bad shepherds, all need love right now. Like my friends remembered in this book, the vast majority of Catholic priests, brothers, and sisters do not prey on children. Instead, they understand and accept this core message of love, they incorporate it into the fabric of their being, and they devote themselves to making the lives of both children and adults better. They are the Word that became flesh and dwelt among us.

■ ■ ■

EPILOGUE
Still Hearing the Bells

LIFE FOR THE MONKS, AND FOR ME, DID NOT END IN 1983 AFTER my post-college retreat at the monastery. Quite a few important things happened after that date.

My beloved monastery is now closed. I did not completely lose contact with the monks after 1983, but as I attended law school, started work, got married, and started a family, time began to fly and the contacts became less frequent. I took Mom and part of my family to the abbey's 50th anniversary celebration in 1997 and introduced my wife and two of our children to many of the monks, including Brother Felix, Father Patrick, Father David, and Brother Boniface. It was a wonderful visit. Some of them also met our children as adults on other later occasions, including during the seventieth year (and last) of the monastery's foundation.

Most of the monks I knew now have gone on to heaven, wearing what Thomas Merton referred to as the Trappist "grim smile of satisfaction." They include: Father Jerome Siler (1987); Father Virgil Dusbabek (1989); Father Andrew Marek (1991); Brother Benedict Castro (1991); Brother Edward Eick (1992); Father Thomas Porter (1997); Father David Kinney (1999); Father Bartholomew Gottemoller (2007); Father Brendan Hanratty (2007); Father Baldwin Shea (2009); Father Joseph Schroer (2010); Brother Felix McHale (2010); Brother Bonaventure Schweiger (2013); Brother Carl Holton (2014); Brother Mark Stazinski (2014); Brother John Peczuh (2016); Father Malachy Flaherty (2018), Brother Nicholas Prinster (2018); Brother Cyril Anderson (2018); Brother David McManus (2019); and Father Charles Cummings (2020). Former Brother Isidore "Izzy" Sullivan also passed away in 2016 at the age of eighty-three.

His friends Brother Nicholas and Father Patrick traveled to Ogden to attend his funeral.

The monks typically do not widely announce when their brothers are sick or pass on, so I learned about nearly all these departures afterwards, sometimes long after they had occurred. After retiring as abbot, serving as a chaplain for some Trappistine nuns, and then returning to Holy Trinity as the guest master, Father Emmanuel Spillane passed away in 2010. At his request, immediately after his burial, his brothers and friends brought ninety-three balloons from the church and released them all, one for each year of his long and fruitful life. He was right. Balloons really do belong in church.

My friend Brother Lawrence (David) Baumbach, one of the youngest members of the monastery, eventually transferred to another Trappist monastery, one with more and younger members, in Genesee, New York. We still write letters to each other. In August 2017, the other surviving Utah monks, most at or near age 90, closed the monastery and moved to St. Joseph's Villa, a Catholic assisted living and medical care facility in nearby Salt Lake City. This group included Father Malachy Flaherty, Brother Nicholas Prinster, Father David Altman, Father Casimir Bernas, Father Leander Dosch, Brother David McManus, and Father Alan Hohl. Their superior at the time, Father Brendan Freeman, helped them with the transition and then started working to try to help save some of the Trappist monasteries in Ireland.

Although he considered a move to Gethsemani Abbey in Kentucky, in order to stay with what he called his "monastic family," Father Patrick also moved to St. Joseph's Villa. He went there with his bags still packed and still ready to go to heaven. In one conversation before he moved, he told me, "Now Mike, I hope you know you always will have a home at Holy Trinity Abbey." I found the statement both poignantly sad and reassuring, sad because even the monks who had lived there seventy years could no longer call the place home, but reassuring because what he really meant is that home is a place in the heart and soul, not in a building or on a certain piece of land.

Brother Boniface's annotated prayer book subtly reveals the story of his own aging process over the three decades that he used the missal. He was in his mid-fifties when I first met him in 1972. He started annotating his prayer book in about 1976, at age 58. In 2000, with the dawn of the new millennium, he noted how twenty-five years had passed by so quickly. His final inscriptions are shaky and must have been written with a trembling hand. The last of these entries simply acknowledged one of his final birthdays with the notation "86...Be." He died soon after, in 2006, at age 87. I did not know at the time, but later I saw a photo of him, in his white cowl, lying still and alone at the bottom of his earthen grave. In contrast to my sad (and youthful) reaction to the death of Father Denis, when I saw the photo I felt only joy for Brother Bon, so maybe I really am part Trappist monk now after all. I am quite certain that his radiant and good face now makes those of the angels themselves pale in comparison.

Pope Francis honored Thomas Merton in the historic address to Congress on September 24, 2015, during his visit to the United States. Merton would have celebrated his 100th birthday in 2015. The Pope highlighted him and three other Americans (President Abraham Lincoln, Dr. Martin Luther King Jr., and Dorothy Day) who "shaped fundamental values which will endure forever in the spirit of the American people." The Pope said of Merton:

A century ago, at the beginning of the Great War, which Pope Benedict XV termed a "pointless slaughter," another notable American was born: the Cistercian monk Thomas Merton. He remains a source of spiritual inspiration and a guide for many people. In his autobiography he wrote: "I came into the world. Free by nature, in the image of God, I was nevertheless the prisoner of my own violence and my own selfishness, in the image of the world into which I was born. That world was the picture of Hell, full of men like myself, loving God, and yet hating him; born to love him, living instead in fear of hopeless self-contradictory hungers". Merton was above all a man of prayer, a thinker who challenged the certitudes of his time and opened new horizons for souls and for the Church. He was also a man of dialogue, a promoter of peace between peoples and religions.[1]

The Pope concluded, "A nation can be considered great when it defends liberty as Lincoln did, when it fosters a culture which enables people to 'dream' of full rights for all their brothers and sisters, as Martin Luther King sought to do; when it strives for justice and the cause of the oppressed, as Dorothy Day did by her tireless work, the fruit of a faith which becomes dialogue and sows peace in the contemplative style of Thomas Merton."[2]

Despite being forced by circumstances onto alternative paths for many years, my sister Karen eventually earned her college degree, got married, had three beautiful daughters, my nieces, the awesome K girls: Katie, Kater, and Kaylin, and moved to Fort Worth, Texas, with her husband, Chip, and their family. Father Chuck Cummins performed Karen's wedding ceremony, and I gave away the bride. Father Chuck also baptized all three of Karen's daughters. When I wrote this book, Father Chuck had remained a priest for almost fifty years and continued to serve the Ogden and Huntsville communities as a chaplain, pastor, coach, and teacher.

My sister Moe also had two wonderful children—boys (now men) Brad and Michael. She showed great courage and compassion in caring for her husband, Warren, before he died of a brain tumor in 2015. My brother Pete had a beautiful daughter, Bonnie, who now is a high school teacher. He eventually retired from the police department, heroic in so many ways, but also scarred by some of the unpleasant things police officers must see and must do.

The fact that I grew up without a father made me want to be one. My wife, Vicki, and I were blessed with three wonderful children, now all adults. Erin Kathleen is a teacher, and in 2016 she provided the occasion for the first family wedding when she married a kind and wonderful fellow teacher named Adam Dahlberg. They gave us our first grandchild in January 2021. Our other daughter, Megan Mary, got her degree in dance and now works as a professional dancer, teacher, and choreographer. Our son, Daniel Patrick, just finished college, studying to be an athletic trainer, and is now beginning to figure out his path. I made sure each met a Trappist monk.

As for me, I graduated from law school in 1986 and have worked with a great law firm—Jones Waldo Holbrook & McDonough in Salt Lake City—since then, practicing media law and employment law. In my employment law work, I help businesses comply with the laws that ensure equal opportunity, civil rights, human dignity, and respect at work. In my media law work, I defend the First Amendment rights of news media outlets, thus helping to ensure freedom of expression and transparency in government and other aspects of public life. I am fortunate that both roles involve noble and worthy activities. As a firm owner, it pleases me to know that our small business employs about 150 people, helping them support and sustain their own families, probably more than 500 people in all.

My father, Kevin, remarried in 1973 and seemed to enjoy some happiness during the last years of his life, but he did not live that long. He contracted hepatitis sometime after the divorce in the late 1970s. It weakened his liver; he developed cancer and passed away in November 1991 at age 60. Before he passed, his second wife called me, told me he was quite sick, and said the end was near. I had not seen or talked with him for a long time, but I decided I should visit him. Unfortunately, I arrived at his home in Roy, Utah, just moments after he died. I guess he and I just never really got in sync with each other.

It was odd for me to attend his nondenominational funeral service because I felt as if I were hearing about a distant acquaintance. Father Chuck later was kind enough to do a small Catholic memorial Mass for him and the family, and all of us were there, except Mom. A few years later, I learned about his secret contributions to my college fund, assisted by Father Draeger. I also received a package from his second wife. She sent me some photos he had taken of me at various events when I had not realized he was there. She also sent a scrapbook he had kept about me, including various newspaper articles about high school and college achievements, and eventually she gave me the 1930s-era typewriter that his father, and my grandfather, used in his writing. Maybe we were not as out of sync as I thought. Maybe it was just a lost opportunity. Whichever the case, our relationship was an enduring life lesson about the sort of father I aspired to be, and desired not to be, for my own children.

Mom lived until 2007, long enough to meet and enjoy all nine of her grandchildren. For the first seventy-five years of her life, she enjoyed good health and never went into a hospital except to have her babies. The last three years were much different. She suffered from congestive heart failure and had bypass surgery in 2005. I helped take care of her until about 2006. I would visit her at home, bring meals by, and tend to the house. Once, while I was cooking for her, she commented, "We've switched roles." Indeed, we had. I had become the caregiver and she, the recipient. I can only hope I did as well in the work as she did. Mom spent the last year of her life living with my sister Karen in Fort Worth. Karen took kind and gentle care of her and was with her when she died. She had broken her hip, and after replacement surgery, she passed away on Easter Monday, April 9, 2007.

Parents teach us so many valuable things, but the last difficult lessons are how to grow old and die. When she passed, I was in Italy on a school-related trip during which we visited the Vatican and saw Pope Benedict, something Mom would have loved to do. It occurred to me later that in her stronger days, with her clever sense of humor, she likely would have told me sarcastically that she would just die if I ever went to see the Pope without her. This thought amused me, because that is exactly what she did.

Like the rest of us sometimes, Mom struggled to pronounce certain words. One was "urn." As she aged, she often told me that when she died, she wanted to be cremated. The thought jolted me, but I think I understand it better now. Like her, when I am gone, I do not want to take up much space, except of course in the hearts and memories of those persons who were kind enough to love me. Mom would also smile and instruct me that after she was cremated, she should be placed in an urn and left on my mantle. However, because she could never quite say "urn," she ended up regularly telling me to put her ashes in "urine." I would laugh at the suggestion and tell her that it really was inappropriate, and that her ashes would not spend time and eternity in urine unless she seriously misbehaved.

When she passed away in 2007, at the suggestion of her brother Jack we took her back home to Burlington, Vermont. We buried her ashes in an emerald-green, marble urn at the same venerable St. Joseph Cemetery gravesite of her beloved uncle, Father Leonard, the man who sang to her and called her his "darling" Kathleen. St. Joseph Cemetery sits on a hill, the oldest Catholic burial ground in Burlington, with interments starting before the Civil War. It is a lovely, spooky, and classic graveyard with narrow dirt roads, and is highlighted by stone gates, mossy obelisks, crooked decaying headstones, and decrepit markers of various shapes and sizes, many of them taller than I am.

It also is a place of great character and great characters. St. Joseph Cemetery has more than 4,000 of Burlington's dearly departed residents, mostly of an Irish Catholic lineage. One of the Irish inhabitants is John Lonergan, a hero from the Battle of Gettysburg and a Civil War Congressional Medal of Honor recipient. Amusingly, Burlington's other main Catholic population of French Canadians primarily are interred in their own segregated fashion, just across the street, in Mount Calvary Cemetery. In life as in death, the two largest Catholic groups exist, or no longer exist, in their own circles.

St. Joseph's is the closest thing I have to a family cemetery, for buried there are three of my grandparents, three sets of great-grandparents, three sets of my great-great-grandparents, and numerous aunts, uncles, cousins several times removed, and assorted other relatives. The grave of Mom's mother, Catherine Sullivan Gleason, in the Leonard family plot had never been properly marked when she died in 1939, or perhaps the original marker had been lost. After Mom's burial in 2007, we included both their names on the same stone grave marker. I think Mom would have liked these decisions.

In a final tribute at her graveside services, we left her with red roses and chocolate-chip cookies, and then invoked her favorite Irish blessing:

May the road rise up to meet you.
May the wind be always at your back.
May the sun shine warm upon your face,
the rains fall soft upon your fields,
and until we meet again,
may God hold you in the palm of his hand.

I remember her every day for many reasons, perhaps best summarized by a little stained glass window she once gave me. It says, "If I could sit across the porch from God, I would thank him for lending you to me." In her final ten years, she enjoyed more peace than she had during the years after the divorce, the greater calm resulting perhaps from being free from the stigma of divorce and the burdens of single parenthood and being unleashed to engage fully in relentless efforts to spoil her grandchildren. When she departed, we shared her small estate with each of them, and thanked God that he had lent her to us for almost eight decades.

As Mom did for me, I have tried to actively introduce my children to good men and women who have devoted themselves to the religious life. One was our parish pastor, Father Dave Van Massenhove, of St. Thomas More Church in Cottonwood Heights, Utah, near Salt Lake City. Although best known as a rabid Green Bay Packers fan, he also is the priest who received the enthusiastic hug from the little girl referred to at the beginning of this book. Another was the very kind Father Terry Moore, yet another priest from Ireland, who baptized two of our three children and was a guest in our home on a couple of occasions. My old friend Monsignor Francis Mannion, the Galway priest for whom I was an altar boy in Ogden, was the pastor at the parish school our kids attended. They also got to meet the man who taught me in eighth grade, Monsignor Joseph Mayo, and Utah Bishop (later San Francisco Archbishop) George Niederauer, a kind and wonderful man who came to dinner at our home on one occasion. Perhaps in a sign of the times, it was not a priest, but a family friend and diocese chancellor, Deacon George Reade, who performed the first family wedding for Erin and Adam.

Despite all this effort, I fear I have not succeeded in this process nearly as well as did my mother. For my children, I hope quality has been more important than quantity. Today priests, nuns, and brothers seem to be a vanishing breed. Upon the foundation of Holy Trinity Abbey in 1947, one writer confidently and optimistically predicted an ongoing upward trend in those choosing a monastic life:

The growth typifies a trend: a trend in America towards monasticism such as occurred before only in the Golden Age in France. Just as St. Robert dared to establish Citeaux and Dom Eutropius Proust Gethsemani, so did Dom Mary Frederic Dunne dare to found Holy Trinity. As Gethsemani proved that the Trappist order could flourish in America, so did Huntsville prove that Cistercians can thrive anywhere in the United States. The picture is clear. The postwar trend is here to stay. Its manifestation in Huntsville was only the first step; and its consistency points unerringly to the fact that the monastic life has earned its niche in our American way of living.[3]

Unfortunately, the experience of Holy Trinity shows the opposite may be true, and not just for the Trappists.

Among Americans today, one of the groups increasing most rapidly in number is that of religiously unaffiliated persons. One out of three Americans age eighteen to twenty-nine belong to this group. The Church seems to rarely be at the center of our lives anymore. So it is no surprise to read that "According to the Center for Applied Research in the Apostolate at Georgetown University, the number of diocesan priests declined from 1965 to 2000 by 15 percent, to 30,607, and the number of nuns and brothers by more than half, to 79,914 and 5,662, respectively."[4] The situation is of such magnitude that in 2017, Pope Francis expressed concern over what he called a "hemorrhage" of priests and nuns from the Catholic Church.[5]

Some of Holy Trinity's fellow Trappist monasteries are experiencing significantly reduced numbers. For example, with only about a dozen elderly monks there, Mepkin Abbey in Moncks Corner, South Carolina, probably is on the verge of closing. New Melleray Abbey in Iowa had one hundred and fifty monks in 1965 but had only three dozen as of five years ago. Even the venerable and longstanding Gethsemani Abbey, which nurtured Thomas Merton and launched Holy Trinity Abbey, has had to adjust its business operations due to a dwindling number of monks there.[6]

These trends certainly affected my monastery. When I started writing this book only about a half-dozen monks lived at Holy Trinity. Their average age was about eighty-five. Perhaps better than most people, the Utah Trappists understood that all human institutions are temporary and fleeting, even when they possess profound meaning, value, and significance that will live on long after the institution itself is gone. On some seventy occasions, on Ash Wednesday every year, the Huntsville monks invoked the iconic Catholic Lenten meditation from Genesis 3:19: "You are dust and to dust you shall return." Although well aware of the looming dust, the monks also understood that Easter lilies always rise from the ashes of Lent.

Thus, although the monks have closed the abbey, they have left the community with a legacy of goodness and kindness comparable to the acts of love they gave while they still lived in Huntsville. The monks shared some of their remaining funds with other monasteries and other good causes. They made contributions to the local Catholic high school and various local Utah charities, including a $400,000 gift to the Lantern House, a homeless shelter, which now bears a large sign acknowledging the monastery and the generous grant. A few years before, the monks made a similar gift to aid in the construction of the shelter facility. Describing the gifts, Father Brendan Freeman, the abbey's final superior, explained: "This was from our blood, sweat, and tears. These men earned money on the farm and never spent it on themselves."

The monks also donated the beautiful Salve window that graced their church for half a century. The spectacular stained-glass window was removed, restored, and re-installed in Holy Family Catholic Church in South Ogden, Utah. The window delighted me as a young boy, and now the lovely image of Mary and her son Jesus will continue to inspire generations of young men and women who get the chance to gaze upon or daydream about it. I visit it when I can, especially at night, when it is illuminated, and its bright colored lights spark memories of my first monastery mornings.

The Utah monks also sold their property to a kind neighbor, a Huntsville water rights attorney named Bill White, in a manner intended to preserve their legacy and the natural beauty of what was their land and home for seven decades. Bill and his wife Alane have been loving and devoted supporters of the Utah monks. Bill is trying to keep most of the land devoted to agriculture and green space. Bill is working with Utah nonprofit conservation associations and others to raise money to put the abbey acreage into a conservation easement that would forever protect it against development.[7] I hope he succeeds.

The monks consulted with graduate students and faculty at Utah's agricultural college, Utah State University in Logan, regarding the best future uses for their land. They and Bill also worked with the Ogden Valley Land Trust and the Summit Land Conservancy on the land preservation issues. The decision to sell, according to a spokesman for the monks, was difficult and made only "after a year and a half of deliberation and prayer." Their Huntsville neighbors understandably were sad. Jody Smith, then-chairwoman of the Ogden Valley Land Trust, said, "It would be nice to have it stay like it is. It's beautiful. They worked all their lives to make it what it is. It started as a patch of sagebrush and they made it what it is today."[8]

Included in the preservation established by the monks and Bill will be the small and quaint cemetery just outside the monastery church, which now is the last earthly resting place of so many of my friends. The thirty or so humble white crosses there are the only tangible reminders of the men who came to Huntsville to live in solitude and pray for the rest of the world. They shall live on in the hearts and memories of those of us who were so blessed to know them and to love them.

Near the end of his autobiography, Merton wrote, "In one sense we are always travelling, and travelling as if we did not know where we are going. In another sense we have already arrived."[9] The Huntsville monks have arrived at the final stage of their seven-decades-long journey that began on a train that left Kentucky on a hot summer morning in 1947. Announcing the closure of the monastery, Father Brendan Freeman concluded his message with these lovely words: "It is our fond hope that future generations will experience not only the beauty of this place but also discern the presence of God, the source of all beauty. There is indeed a presence of the Holy in the hills and valleys, the sky and mountains sitting so majestically right before our eyes in the Ogden Valley. May it always be so."[10]

While sitting quietly at home, in what has fast become the evening of my lifetime, I have the solitude to cherish the many profound boyhood hours I spent there. One beloved memory is hearing the bells of the monks' church. The bell tower rose fifteen feet above the roof of their simple Quonset hut monastery and included one large bell and two smaller ones. The bells rang out several times each day, announcing the monastic morning and Trappist twilight, and many of the most important moments in between. I heard them ring hundreds of times.

With the monastery now closed, those lovely bells are silent. Or are they?

One of the monks, Brother Nicholas Prinster, listened to those same monastery bells every day for more than fifty years. Unable to farm or to ranch as the years passed, Brother Nicholas turned to woodworking in his old age, to keep busy, to contribute to the well-being of his brothers, and to proclaim the goodness of God with the beautiful work of his hands. Among other things, he made wooden clocks. And within each one of his clocks, he included bells.

I visited the abbey, Brother Nicholas's home, and my own home-away-from-home, for the last time in August 2017, just before it closed. It was my final monastery morning.

I sat alone in the church and watched the colored lights of the stained glass window dance in perfect synchronicity with the silent echoes of seventy years of monk voices raised in chant.

I walked down the tree-lined Abbey Road. The road cuts a path between two of the fields, both abundantly filled on that day with a late summer growth of alfalfa hay. I saw dozens of small white butterflies gently fluttering between the fragrant green plants. It was a dreamlike vision, almost as if all my boyhood memories had taken to winged flight just so they and I could be together, quietly and one last time, in that lovely place where we had first met.

The last thing I did was buy one of Brother Nicholas's clocks. It might be the very last one he made. Built from chestnut brown wood, it is about eighteen inches tall, just over a foot wide, with a brass-trimmed clock face that shows the time in classic Roman numerals. And, of course, it has bells.

Four times an hour and forty-eight times a day, those bells chime softly in my home. They announce my morning, my twilight, and many of the most important moments in between. They blend seamlessly with my beating heart, resurrecting the music of the bells I heard and loved so many decades ago when I first discovered the point of stillness in my perpetually turning world.

■ ■ ■

ACKNOWLEDGMENTS

Many hands, hearts, and minds made this book possible, but none more so than my family. Perhaps it goes without saying, but I appreciate that my mother brought me to the Huntsville Trappist monastery, among so many other things she did for me. Thank you, family—Vicki Comeau O'Brien, Megan O'Brien, Danny O'Brien, Erin O'Brien Dahlberg, and Adam Dahlberg—for reading, advice, and encouragement. I appreciate my sisters Karen O'Brien Taylor and Moe O'Brien Ferree for helping me remember the life events we shared. I love you all!

My agent Joseph Durepos, my editor Jon M. Sweeney, and Jon's wonderful team at Paraclete Press took a chance on a rookie author like me. I am forever grateful for their kindness, professional expertise, hard work, and support. They made this book better than I ever imagined it could be. I never would have met any of them if Chicago book publicist Kelly Hughes had not referred me to Joe, and I never would have met Kelly but for her friend and my law partner Jim Peters. Thank you!

I appreciate my work colleague Vickie Christensen Smoot, who never refused when I asked her to read a new version of the evolving book or to proofread something. My friend Lisa Carricaburu encouraged me and gave the book a much-needed professional edit before I sent it out to possible publishers. I appreciate Bill White from Huntsville, for reading a draft of this book and for trying to preserve the open lands of the monastery as a legacy to the monks. I also am grateful to my law firm, Jones Waldo Holbrook and McDonough, for allowing me to use firm equipment/resources to research and write. I thank my Jones Waldo law partners Keven Rowe, Angus Edwards, Daniel Daines, and Brent Winder for helping me with various legal issues related to publishing.

The following persons were kind enough to read versions or parts of this book and suggest changes: Connie and Bill Saccomanno, George Reade (chancellor for the Diocese of Salt Lake City); Father David Altman,

OCSO; Jathan Janove; Mark Tolman; Jesse Oakeson; Reid L. Neilson from the History Department of The Church of Jesus Christ of Latter-day Saints; Ann Cannon; Terry Orme; Betsy Burton ("Don't write like a lawyer!"); Erin Wynn; Monsignor M. Francis Mannion; Father Charles Cummins; Gary Topping; Marianna Hopkins; and Brother Luke Armour, OCSO, of Gethsemani Abbey in Kentucky. Thank you for helping me.

I could not have completed the necessary research for this project without the valued help of Gary Topping, archivist for the Diocese of Salt Lake City; LaVon Allen, Velma Ahlstrom, and Gail Ahlstrom, historians at the Huntsville History Library; Father Brendan Freeman, OCSO; Don Morrissey, volunteer library assistant at Holy Trinity Abbey; Kathleen Messier, archivist for the Diocese of Burlington, Vermont; Father William R. Beaudin, pastor of the Assumption of the Blessed Virgin Mary parish in Middlebury, Vermont; Shane MacDonald, archives technician, and Paul Kelly, digital archivist, both at The Catholic University of America; Dirk Bailey, for some stories about the monks and the saints; Google; Newspapers.com; and Ancestry.com. I also appreciate the encouragement from my parish priest, Father John Evans.

Finally, I thank all the Catholic priests, monks, and nuns who cared about me and who took me under their wings, especially the Huntsville, Utah, Trappist monks. They did so not because I would someday mention them in a book, but because they are men and women of love. In turn, I have loved telling their—our—story.

NOTES

CHAPTER 1 Still Point

1 These words come from Thomas Stearns Eliot's famous work "Four Quartets." See "T.S. Eliot's Little Gidding," http://www.columbia.edu/itc/history/winter/w3206/edit/tseliotlittlegidding.html. The specific line is from his final "quartet" called "Little Gidding," which Eliot finished in 1942, and is about a former small Anglican monastery or religious community in Little Gidding. Perhaps this is why the quote was included in the monastery's brochure.

CHAPTER 2 Good Turns

1 Randolph T. Holhut, "The Green Wave," *The Commons Online*, March 16, 2001, citing Vincent E. Feeney, *Finnegans, Slaters and Stonepeggers: A History of the Irish in Vermont* (Bennington, VT: Images from the Past, 2009).

2 Feeney, *Finnegans*, 21–22; Anonymous [Nathaniel Hawthorne], "The Inland Port," *The New-England Magazine* 9 (December 1835): 398–409.

3 Mokyr, Joel, "Great Famine," Encyclopedia Brittanica, last modified February 4, 2020, http://www.britannica.com/event/Great-Famine-Irish-history; "Number of Irish Americans seven times larger than entire population of Ireland," Irish Central, http://www.irishcentral.com/news/census-shows-almost-seven-times-more-irish-americans-than-population-of-ireland-218344001-237779801.html

4 Holhut, "The Green Wave," citing Feeney, *Finnegans*.

5 "Jets Roar Where Field Mice Slept," *The Deseret News*, November 6, 1965.

CHAPTER 5 Near to Heaven

1 Author unknown (believed to be a Trappist), "The Coming of the Trappists to Utah." (copy on file); Rev. M. Raymond, OCSO, *The Less Traveled Road - a memoir of Dom Mary Frederic Dunne, OCSO, First American Trappist Abbot* (Milwaukee: The Bruce Publishing Company, 1953), 9–10.

2 Thomas Merton, "The Trappists Go to Utah," in *Thomas Merton Early Essays 1947-1952*, ed. Patrick F. O'Connell (Collegeville, MN: Liturgical Press, 2015), 19–20. This is an essay that Merton, a monk at Gethsemani, submitted for publication in *Commonweal* magazine on August 29, 1947.

3 "Abbey of the Holy Trinity," July 1997 photo brochure published by the Monastery on its 50th Anniversary; Kathryn L. MacKay, "Sisters of Ogden's Mount Benedict Monastery," *Utah Historical Quarterly* 77 (Summer 2009): 248, n. 15.

4 Raymond, *The Less Traveled Road*, 224, 237, 243–44.

5 "Ogden Stockyards and Meat Packing Industry," last updated January 2, 2018, http://utahrails.net/industries/livestock-ogden.php; Fr. Charles Cummings, OCSO, "A Monk Talks to Mormons," Holy Trinity unpublished pamphlet, November 1978 (copy on file); "Abbey of the Holy Trinity," July 1997 photo brochure published by the Monastery on its fiftieth Anniversary; Stephen Dark, "The World is Their Cloister," *City Weekly*, May 11, 2006; Raymond, *The Less Traveled Road*, 224, 240–41.

6 Lynn Arave, "The Mystery of Monte Cristo," *The Deseret News*, June 21, 1996.

7 Merton, "The Trappists Go to Utah," 19.

8 Author unknown, "Our Lady of the Holy Trinity - Historical Notes and Sketches," 1947 (copy on file). This is a travel log written by an unknown author, one of the monks who made the trip from Gethsemani.

9 Merton, "The Trappists Go to Utah," 21.

10 Author unknown, "Historical Notes and Sketches."

11 Author unknown, "Historical Notes and Sketches."

12 "Trappists Greeted Upon Arrival From Kentucky," *Ogden Standard-Examiner*, July 11, 1947.

13 Merton, "The Trappists Go to Utah," 25. Guinness bought the Schenley liquor company in 1987. Steve Lohr, "Guinness Agrees to Buy Schenley from Riklis," *New York Times*, September 18, 1987.

14 T. E. Johnson, "Trappist Unit Starts Life of Sacrifices," *The Salt Lake Tribune*, November 2, 1947; Author unknown, "Historical Notes and Sketches."

15 "Trappists Greeted Upon Arrival From Kentucky," *Ogden Standard-Examiner*, July 11, 1947.

16 Author unknown, "Historical Notes and Sketches."

17 Author unknown, "Historical Notes and Sketches."

18 "Officials Greeted at Monastery in Ogden Valley," *Ogden Standard-Examiner*, July 11, 1949.

19 "Monastery Ready for Cold Days," *Ogden Standard-Examiner*, October 19, 1947; Fr. Brendan Freeman, OCSO, "Huntsville Abbey has been sold," *Intermountain Catholic*, October 30, 2015.

20 Author unknown, "Historical Notes and Sketches."

21 "Catholics Plan New Center," *The Salt Lake Tribune*, January 16, 1949.

22 Johnson, "Trappist Unit"; Raymond, *The Less Traveled Road*, 9–10.

23 Alfred Gladwell, "Monks Will Build $30 Million Monastery East of Huntsville," *The Ogden Standard-Examiner*, February 29, 1952.

24 Gladwell, "Monks Will Build $30 Million Monastery East of Huntsville."

25 Merton, "The Trappists Go to Utah," 23–24.

26 "Monastery Defers Construction of Abbey Quarters," *Ogden Standard-Examiner*, September 23, 1964.

27 "Abbey of Our Lady of the Holy Trinity," http://www.holytrinityabbey.org/history.html

28 "Cistercians," Wikipedia, last updated July 14, 2020, https://en.wikipedia.org/wiki/Cistercians#cite_note-2, citing *The American Heritage Dictionary of the English Language*, 3rd ed., 1992.

29 Dante Alighieri, *The Divine Comedy*, trans. Henry Wadsworth Longfellow (New York: Fall River Press, 2013), 688–93.

30 "Monastic Life at Abbey of the Holy Trinity," 1990 brochure produced by the Monastery (copy on file).

31 Abbey of Our Lady of the Holy Trinity, http://www.holytrinityabbey.org/history.html.

32 "Rule of Benedict," https://www.ocso.org/resources/foundational-text/rule-of-st-benedict/; Anthony C. Meisel and M. L. del Mastro, *The Rule of St. Benedict* (Garden City, NY: Image Books, 1975), 11.

33 Meisel and del Mastro, Chapter (Rule) 4 in *Rule of St. Benedict*, 52–53.

34 Meisel and del Mastro, Chapter (Rule) 73 in *Rule of St. Benedict*, 106.

35 Meisel and del Mastro, Chapter (Rule) 30 in *Rule of St. Benedict*, 74.

36 "Abbey of the Holy Trinity," 1972 brochure produced by the monks of Holy Trinity Abbey (copy on file) (hereafter "1972 Monastery Brochure").

37 "Gethsemani," Order of Cistercians of the Strict Observance, http://www.ocso.org/index.php?option=com_mtree&task=viewlink&link_id=2377&Itemid=88&lang=en.

38 Gustav Niebuhr, "Recruiting Pitch: Monastic Life, for 3 Days," *New York Times*, January 13, 2001.

39 "Men Choosing the Monastic Life, after World War II and Today," (Emory University interview of Fr. Matthew Torpley, OCSO, dated March 11, 2015), https://www.youtube.com/watch?v=4VdMqgnsCAA.

40 Jonathan Petre, "Monks and their monasteries go into retreat as recruits dwindle," *The Telegraph*, April 10, 2006.

41 Freeman, "Huntsville Abbey has been sold."

42 Dark, "The World is Their Cloister."

43 Cummings, "A Monk Talks to Mormons."

44 1972 Monastery Brochure.

45 Cummings, "A Monk Talks to Mormons."

46 Boniface, Brother, an oral history by Randee Minnoch, 07 May 1972, WSU Stewart Library Oral History Program, University Archives, Stewart Library, Weber State University, Ogden, UT (hereafter "Brother Boniface Oral History").

47 Hilary Groutage, "Keeping the faith - Huntsville Monks Pray For the World - But Who Will Carry On After Them?" *The Salt Lake Tribune*, June 15, 1997.

CHAPTER 6 First Friends

1 Jeremias Drexelius, *Heliotropium - Conformity of the Human Will to the Divine* (New York: The Devin-Adair Company, Second Printing 1958), 3.

2 James J. Rue and Louise Shanahan, *The Divorced Catholic* (Paramus, NJ: Paulist Press, 1972), 2.

3 Eduardo Bonnín and Francisco Forteza, "Evangelization through Conversion," National Cursillo Movement, https://www.natl-cursillo.org/eduardo-bonnin-aguilo/evangelization-through-conversion/aguilo/evangelization-through-conversion/

4 See de Colores from *Romero*, https://www.youtube.com/watch?v=cPi2PnpYQok.

5 "The Rev. Thomas Meersman Dies," *The Deseret News*, September 23, 1991.

6 Fr. David Altman, OCSO, *The Value of Monasticism*, April 25, 2007, Abbey of the Holy Trinity "Monksword," http://www.holytrinityabbey.org/monksword.html.

7 "A Monk's Day," Abbey of the Holy Trinity, http://www.holytrinityabbey.org/monksday.html.

8 "St. Benedict's Monastery," http://www.snowmass.org/

9 Meisel and del Mastro, *Rule of St. Benedict*, Chapter 63, 98–99, Chapter 71, 105.

10 "Priest will enter Trappist Order," *Los Angeles Times*, January 10, 1950; "Hollywood Priest Begins Stay at Valley Monastery," *Ogden Standard-Examiner*, February 3, 1950.

11 Many of these details are in his obituary, which can be found at http://www.icatholic.org/article/former-abbot-of-the-abbey-of-our-lady-of-the-holy-trinity-671807. A list of all the abbots at Holy Trinity is available here: http://www.ocso.org/index.php?option=com_mtree&task=viewlink&link_id=2386&Itemid=88&lang=en.

12 George Fowler, *Dance of a Fallen Monk* (Reading, MA: Addison Wesley Publishing Co., 1995), 149.

13 Thomas Merton, *Dancing in the Water of Life: Seeking Peace in the Hermitage*, ed. Robert E. Daggy (HarperCollins e-books), https://archive.org/stream/ThomasMerton_201710/%5BThomas_Merton%5D_Dancing_in_the_Water_of_Life(BookFi)_djvu.txt.

14 You can listen to a great version of the song here at "Song of Good News Father Willard Jabusch," https://www.youtube.com/watch?v=E3F9Mr0NvEg.

15 You can read the poem at "Thinking Out Loud," http://fourthof9.blogspot.com/2011/12/balloons-belong-in-church-by-ann-weems.html.

16 Thomas Merton, *The Seven Storey Mountain* (New York: Harcourt, Brace and Company, 1948), 263. I salvaged a re-bound 1948 first print edition of this book from the Monastery library. Somehow, it seemed appropriate to use that edition of Merton's work for this book rather than later paperback editions.

17 Fowler, *Dance of a Fallen Monk*, 106.

18 Lois M. Collins, "Seeking God," *The Deseret News*, July 12, 1997.

19 Peter Anderson, *First Church of the Higher Elevations: Mountains, Prayer and Presence* (Golden, CO: Conundrum Press, 2015), https://books .GMKHeAECB84ChDoAQgpMAM#v=onepage&q=abbey%20holy%20trinity%20 utah&f=false.

20 Jack Goodman, "Trappist monastery utilizes war time Quonset huts." *The Salt Lake Tribune*, February 16, 1992.

21 "The Orator's Gestures," http://www.romanmysteries.com/sites/romanmysteries.com/ files/cms_images/gesturesoftheorator.jpg.

22 You can view a photo of the spectacular window here: https://cabledsheep.files .wordpress.com/2013/08/abbey2.jpg.

23 Johnson, "Trappist Unit;" Robbin Devine, "Closeness to God Gives Purpose to Monastic Life," *Ogden Standard-Examiner*, April 16, 1969.

24 Collins, "Seeking God."

25 "Bookstore and Gift Shop," Abbey of the Holy Trinity, http://www.holytrinityabbey.org/ store.html.

26 This is promoted as a special make-it-at-home recipe at "100% whole wheat bread," http://www.food.com/recipe/100-whole-wheat-bread-82530.

27 *The Washington Post* has published a full transcript of the Pope's speech at: "Transcript: Pope Francis's Speech to Congress," https://www.washingtonpost.com/local/social -issues/transcript-pope-franciss-speech-to-congress/2015/09/24/6d7d7ac8-62bf-11e5 -8e9e-dce8a2a2a679_story.html.

28 Dorothy Day, "On Pilgrimage," *The Catholic Worker*, September 1978, available at http://www.catholicworker.org/dorothyday/articles/591.pdf.

29 Holy Trinity Abbey Cream Honey brochure, undated (copy on file).

30 Photo from *Ogden Standard-Examiner*, December 2, 1994.

31 Mel Reisner, "In case of nuclear attack, monks have a 'honey' of a shelter," *Ogden Standard-Examiner*, December 13, 1971.

32 Stephen Matlow, "Rites of Voting," *Ogden Standard-Examiner*, November 4, 1980.

33 "NIR-ARMAGH-L Archives," http://archiver.rootsweb.ancestry.com/th/read/NIR -ARMAGH/2002-02/1014348492ARMAGH/2002-02/1014348492.

34 I obtained background information about the monks that I did not already know from various obituaries published about them.

35 Kristen Moulton, "Saying Goodbye to Brother Felix," *The Salt Lake Tribune*, March 16, 2012.

36 Bert Strand, "Ogden Elk Herds Prove Interesting Visitors at Abbey," *Ogden Standard-Examiner*, May 2, 1965.

37 Strand, "Ogden Elk Herds Prove Interesting Visitors at Abbey."

38 Merton, *The Seven Storey Mountain*, 419.

CHAPTER 7 Brother Good Face

1 Becky Wright, "Historian says 25th Street's notorious reputation more about religion than prostitutes," *Ogden Standard-Examiner*, October 13, 2013.

2 Ralph Whitesides, "How to Take the Bite Out of Puncturvine," May 16, 2012, Utah State University Extension, https://extension.usu.edu/archive/how-to-take-the-bite- out-of -puncturvine

3 Myers Mortuary, http://www.myers-mortuary.com/obituary/Boniface-Milton -Ptasienski/Huntsville-UT/287320Ptasienski/Huntsville-UT/287320.

4 Brother Boniface Oral History.

5 Merton, *The Seven Storey Mountain*, 372.

6 Brother Boniface Oral History.

7 Lon LaFlamme, "Valley Monks Begin 25th Year - Devoted to 'Cause,'" *Ogden Standard-Examiner*, October 8, 1972.

8 Author Unknown, "Historical Notes and Sketches."

9 The missal is *New St. Joseph Weekday Missal Complete Edition* (New York: Catholic Book Publishing Company, 1975).

10 Brother Boniface Oral History.

11 John M. Young, "No Time Waste at Abbey Farm," *Ogden Standard-Examiner*, January 30, 1966; Devine, "Closeness to God."

12 Strand, "Ogden Elk Herds Prove Interesting Visitors at Abbey"; "Second of Three," *Ogden Standard-Examiner*, November 24, 1964; "Abbey Wages Rodent Drive to Save Crop," *Ogden Standard-Examiner*, May 3, 1965.

13 Mark 12:43–44.

14 Brother Boniface Oral History.

15 Jerry L. Croasman, "I Likes This," http://www.devotionsfordevelopment.com/likes.htm.

CHAPTER 8 The Slowest Superhero

1 Rev. Lawrence G. Lovasik, *New Picture Book of Saints* (New York: Catholic Book Publishing Company, 1970), n.p.

2 Revelation 12:1–9.

3 You can see several excellent photos of Fr. Patrick at "The monastic life: Dispensing wisdom in a confusing world (23 photos)," http://m.deseretnews.com/photo/865616607?nm=1.

4 Sharalee Huntsman, "24 Monks Live in Monastery in Huntsville," *The Digital Universe*, April 30, 1997.

5 J. J. Despain, "Monastery invites all to learn about Catholicism," *The Daily Universe*, June 15, 2010.

6 Despain, "Monastery invites all to learn about Catholicism."

7 "Abbey of the Holy Trinity- Historical Documentary," John Koenig Production, 2013. Copy available in archives of Diocese of Salt Lake City.

8 Paige Wiren, "Trappist Monastery in Eden, Utah," *Utah Stories*, April 25, 2012.

9 Jerry Johnston, "Monk's Life is Full of Hope," *The Deseret News*, April 8, 2000.

CHAPTER 9 Chasing Cows

1 "A Monk's Day," Holy Trinity Abbey, http://www.holytrinityabbey.org/monksday.html.

2 Merton, *The Seven Storey Mountain*, 413.

3 Meisel and del Mastro, Chapter (Rule) 66 in *Rule of St. Benedict*, 102.

4 Moulton, "Saying Goodbye to Brother Felix."

5 Barbara Stinson Lee, "Philadelphia-born priest becomes sixth abbot," *Intermountain Catholic*, July 27, 2007.

6 "Our Life," Order of Cistercians of the Strict Observance, http://www.ocso.org/index.php?option=com_content&view=article&id=92&Itemid=108&lang=en.

CHAPTER 10 The Seasons of Abbey Life

1 Merton, *The Seven Storey Mountain*, 389.

2 Ecclesiastes 3:1.

3 Meisel and del Mastro, Chapter (Rule) 58 in *Rule of St. Benedict*, 93.

4 This path is described in more detail at "Becoming a monk or nun," Order of Cistercians of the Strict Observance, https://www.ocso.org/who-we-are/becoming-a-monk-or-nun/.

5 "Becoming a monk or nun," http://www.ocso.org/index.php?option=com_content&view=article&id=51&Itemid=61&lang=en.

6 Donna Lou Morgan, "Sweet Side of Life…Monastery Honey," *The Salt Lake Tribune*, March 24, 1993.

7 1972 Monastery Brochure.

8 Merton, *The Seven Storey Mountain*, 421.

9 Fowler, *Dance of a Fallen Monk*, 117–18.

10 Merton, *The Seven Storey Mountain*, 389.

11 Larry Evans, "Monk's Life Not for You? He Wouldn't Trade Either," *Ogden Standard-Examiner*, September 7, 1952.

12 Karl Cates, "Grave Images: The dead and their resting places have poignant tales to tell," *The Deseret News*, May 29, 1994.

13 Thomas Merton, "Death of a Trappist," in *Thomas Merton Early Essays 1947-1952*, ed. Patrick F. O'Connell (Collegeville, MN: Liturgical Press, 2015), 81.

14 Moulton, "Saying Goodbye to Brother Felix."

CHAPTER 11 Monastic Winter

1 "Cold? Forget It! Huntsville Mercury Plummets to 40 below Zero," *Ogden Standard-Examiner*, February 1, 1951. Average annual Huntsville temperature and snowfall averages can be found at "U.S. Climate Data," http://www.usclimatedata.com/climate/huntsville/utah/united-states/usut0117. Other demographics about Huntsville (such as elevation) are available at "Huntsville Town- Demographics," http://huntsvilletown.com/demographics/.

2 Thomas Merton, *No Man is an Island* (New York: Harcourt, Brace and Company, 1955),127.

3 Isaiah 9:6; Luke 2:1–21.

CHAPTER 12 Monks and Saints

1 "Huntsville Town History - Founding," http://huntsvilletown.com/history/.

2 Huntsman, "24 Monks Live in Monastery in Huntsville."

3 Moulton, "Saying Goodbye to Brother Felix."

4 Moulton, "Saying Goodbye to Brother Felix."

5 Author Unknown, "Historical Notes and Sketches."

6 Brother Boniface Oral History.

7 Gregory A. Prince and Wm. Robert Wright, *David O. McKay and the Rise of Modern Mormonism* (Salt Lake City: University of Utah Press, 2005) 112–126. Specifically, they address this issue regarding the Catholic Church in Chapter 5 "Ecumenical Outreach."

8 Gregory A. Prince and Gary Topping, "A Turbulent Coexistence: Duane Hunt, David O. McKay, and a Quarter Century of Catholic-Mormon Relations," *Journal of Mormon History* 31 (Spring 2005): 142–63; Prince and Wright, *David O. McKay*, 120–21.

9 Author Unknown, "Historical Notes and Sketches."

10 Prince and Wright, *David O. McKay*, 122.

11 Prince and Wright, *David O. McKay*, 123.

12 Prince and Wright, *David O. McKay*, 123.

13 Moulton, "Saying Goodbye to Brother Felix."

14 Neil K. Newell, "Pure Religion: Fresh-baked bread," *Church News - The Church of Jesus Christ of Latter-day Saints*, June 16, 2001; Moulton, "Saying Goodbye to Brother Felix."

15 Groutage, "Keeping the Faith."

16 Kristen Moulton, "Ogden Valley's Trappist Monks celebrate new abbot," *The Salt Lake Tribune*, August 30, 2007; Despain, "Monastery invites all to learn about Catholicism."

17 Newell, "Pure Religion: Fresh-baked bread."

18 Newell, "Pure Religion: Fresh-baked bread."

19 "Bridging the Religious Divide: Open Letter to the Community," *The Deseret News,* January 21, 2006; Derek P. Jensen, "Next SLC Mayor Faces Prickly Question: The Religious Divide," *The Salt Lake Tribune,* September 1, 2007.

20 "The Unspoken Divide," *The Salt Lake Tribune,* December 9, 2001.

21 "Bridging the Religious Divide: Open Letter to the Community," *The Deseret News.*

CHAPTER 13 Fellow Pilgrims Seeking Light

1 Meisel and del Mastro, Chapter (Rule) 53 in *Rule of St. Benedict,* 89.

CHAPTER 14 Discordant Notes in the Choir

1 Merton, *The Seven Storey Mountain,* 379.

2 Merton, *The Seven Storey Mountain,* 381.

3 Thomas Merton, *The School of Charity: Letters on Religious Renewal and Spiritual Direction,* ed. Patrick Hart, (New York: Farrar, Straus, Giroux, 1990), 96–98.

4 Merton, *The School of Charity,* 96–98.

5 "Prophet sentenced to Jail," *Ogden Standard-Examiner,* December 5, 1972; see also "Jury Convicts Prophet on Charges of Battery," *Ogden Standard-Examiner,* November 30, 1972; "Judge gives probation to Ogdenite," *Ogden Standard-Examiner,* December 9, 1973.

6 Altman, *The Value of Monasticism.*

7 Merton, *The Seven Storey Mountain,* 215. For more information on Hopkins, see "Gerard Manley Hopkins," Poetry Foundation, http://www.poetryfoundation.org/bio/gerard-manley-hopkins.

8 Charles F. Trentelman, "The life of a monk is not the same as being a monk for life," *Ogden Standard-Examiner,* July 31, 2010.

9 Alex Harrington, "Fr. Charles Cummins celebrates 80th birthday and 44 years of service in Utah," *Intermountain Catholic,* April 28, 2017; Marie Mischel, "Fr. Charles Cummins recognized for years of service to Utah Catholic education," *Intermountain Catholic,* May 26, 2017; JaNae Francis, "Ogden-area priest receives Christ the Teacher Award for educational leadership," *Ogden Standard-Examiner,* April 3, 2017; Bob Mims, "Utah Catholics honor Weber State's do-everything Father Cummins," *The Salt Lake Tribune,* March 17, 2017.

10 I read a wonderful 80th birthday notice from 2012 about Izzy here: Charles T. "Izzy" Sullivan Jr., http://www.standard.net/stories/2012/01/16/charles-t-izzy-sullivan-jr. You can read his obituary here: http://www.myers-mortuary.com/obituary/Charles-Izzy-Thomas-Sullivan-Jr./Clinton-UT/1577777.

11 Meisel and del Mastro, Chapter (Rule) 29 in *Rule of St. Benedict,* 73–74.

12 Trentelman, "The life of a monk is not the same as being a monk for life."

CHAPTER 15 The Unwanted Lineup

1 Kurt Kragthorpe, "Tommy Lasorda, Steve Garvey, Bill Buckner: All of their careers were launched in 1968 in Ogden," *The Salt Lake Tribune,* July 24, 2018.

2 "Fr. Draeger Dies Following Surgery," *Intermountain Catholic,* August 21, 1981.

3 Msgr. William H. MacDougall, "Fr. Draeger Was a Priest's Priest," *Intermountain Catholic,* August 21, 1981.

CHAPTER 16 A Saint among the Saints

1 "The Nobel Peace Prize 1979" (announcement press release, October 27, 1979), The Nobel Prize, accessed June 10, 2016, http://www.nobelprize.org/nobel_prizes/peace/laureates/1979/press.html.

2 Malcolm Muggeridge, *Something Beautiful for God* (New York: Ballentine Books, 1971), 125.

3 Muggeridge, *Something Beautiful for God*, 88.

4 Mark Zoellner, "Chanting the Days - Huntsville's Trappist Monastery," *Northern Utah Junction*, February 1998.

5 A general finding aid for these archives, including the tapes, is available at: http://archives.lib.cua.edu/findingaid/teresa.cfm, and hereafter, the tapes from these archives will be referred to as "Mother Teresa Huntsville Visit 1972 tapes (copy on file)." Any quotes in the paragraphs that follow are Mother Teresa's words from these 1972 tapes.

6 "Need for Jesus Stressed Here by Visiting Catholic," *Ogden Standard-Examiner*, November 11, 1972.

7 Muggeridge, *Something Beautiful for God*, 146.

8 Michael Patrick O'Brien, "Op-ed: When Mother Teresa came to Utah 44 years ago, the monks knew she would be a saint," *The Salt Lake Tribune*, September 3, 2016.

CHAPTER 17 College and Vocation

1 "Principal Appointed at St. Joseph High," *Ogden Standard-Examiner*, January 29, 1977; "Ogden School Denies Rumors of Closing," *The Salt Lake Tribune*, September 3, 1977.

2 Fr. Jerome's obituary was published in the *Intermountain Catholic* on January 1, 1988.

3 "The Mariological Society of America Bylaws," The Mariological Society of America, http://www.mariologicalsociety.com/BylawsAmended2011.pdf.

4 You can watch the monks chant this psalm at: "Monastery Videos," http://www.holytrinityabbey.org/prayers.html.

CHAPTER 18 A Boy Monk's Vows

1 John 1:1, 1:14.

2 *Catechism of the Catholic Church* (New York: Catholic Book Publishing Company, 1994), 115–117.

3 Emily Stimpson Chapman, "Understanding the Dark Night of the Soul," *Our Sunday Visitor*, May 20, 2015.

4 Cindy Wooden, "Pope Francis says doubt is key to life of faith," *Catholic News Service*, November 23, 2016.

5 Richard P. McBrien, *Catholicism* (Minneapolis: Winston Press, 1980) 477.

6 "Jesus Is Human Face of God, Divine Face of Man, Says Pope," *Zenit.org*, January 11, 2004, https://zenit.org/articles/jesus-is-human-face-of-god-and-divine-face-of-man-says-pope/.

7 "Becoming a Trappist monk or nun - the Vows," Order of Cistercians of the Strict Observance, http://www.trappists.org/becoming-trappist/vows (hereafter "Trappist Website - Description of Vows").

8 1972 Monastery Brochure.

9 Trappist Website - Description of Vows.

10 "Hupakouo," http://www.biblestudytools.com/lexicons/greek/nas/hupakouo.html.

11 Trappist Website - Description of Vows.

12 Dorothy Day, *The Long Loneliness* (San Francisco: Harper & Row, 1952), 286.

13 Trappist Website - Description of Vows.

14 Trappist Website - Description of Vows.

15 Trappist Website - Description of Vows.

16 This quote is from his 1942 poem, see "T. S. Eliot's *Little Gidding*," http://www.columbia .edu/itc/history/winter/w3206/edit/tseliotlittlegidding.html.

17 McBrien, *Catholicism*, 710–14, 726.

EPILOGUE Still Hearing the Bells

1 *The Washington Post* has published a full transcript of the Pope's speech at: "Transcript, Pope Francis's Speech to Congress," https://www.washingtonpost.com /local/social-issues/transcript-pope-franciss-speech-to-congress/2015/09/24/6d7d7ac8 -62bf-11e5-8e9e-dce8a2a2a679_story.html.

2 Transcript, Pope Francis's Speech to Congress.

3 Author unknown, "The Coming of the Trappists to Utah."

4 Niebuhr, "Recruiting Pitch: Monastic Life, for 3 Days."

5 Associated Press, "Pope Frets About 'Hemorrhage' of Priests, Nuns From Church," http://hosted.ap.org/dynamic/stories/E/EU_REL_ VATICAN_FEWER_PRIESTS?SITE=AP&SECTION=HOME& TEMPLATE=DEFAULT&CTIME=2017-01-28-08-27-48.

6 Robert P. Jones, *The End of White Christian America* (New York: Simon & Schuster: 2016), 47–48; Fr. Brendan Freeman, OCSO, "Huntsville Abbey Sold," Ogden Valley News, November 15, 2015; Stephen Hiltner, "The World Is Changing. This Trappist Abbey Isn't. Can It Last?" *The New York Times*, March 17, 2018; John Burger, "Gethsemani Abbey, where Merton lived, makes major change," https://aleteia .org/2016/07/23/abbey-where-thomas-merton-lived-makes-major-change/?utm_ campaign=english_page&utm_medium=aleteia_en&utm_source=Facebook.

7 Mitch Shaw, "Huntsville man on a mission to preserve monastery open space," *Ogden Standard-Examiner*, April 12, 2017.

8 Jesus Lopez Jr., "What Does the Future Hold?" *Ogden Standard-Examiner*, March 8, 2015.

9 Merton, *The Seven Storey Mountain*, 419.

10 Freeman, "Huntsville Abbey has been sold."Raymond, *The Less Traveled Road*, 224, 240–41.

ABOUT PARACLETE PRESS

Who We Are

As the publishing arm of the Community of Jesus, Paraclete Press presents a full expression of Christian belief and practice—from Catholic to Evangelical, from Protestant to Orthodox, reflecting the ecumenical charism of the Community and its dedication to sacred music, the fine arts, and the written word. We publish books, recordings, sheet music, and video/DVDs that nourish the vibrant life of the church and its people.

What We Are Doing

BOOKS | PARACLETE PRESS BOOKS show the richness and depth of what it means to be Christian. While Benedictine spirituality is at the heart of who we are and all that we do, our books reflect the Christian experience across many cultures, time periods, and houses of worship.

We have many series, including *Paraclete Essentials*; *Raven* (fiction); *Iron Pen* (poetry); *Paraclete Giants*; for children and adults, *All God's Creatures*, books about animals and faith; and *San Damiano Books*, focusing on Franciscan spirituality. Others include *Voices from the Monastery* (men and women monastics writing about living a spiritual life today), *Active Prayer*, and new for young readers: *The Pope's Cat*. We also specialize in gift books for children on the occasions of Baptism and First Communion, as well as other important times in a child's life, and books that bring creativity and liveliness to any adult spiritual life.

The MOUNT TABOR BOOKS series focuses on the arts and literature as well as liturgical worship and spirituality; it was created in conjunction with the Mount Tabor Ecumenical Centre for Art and Spirituality in Barga, Italy.

MUSIC | PARACLETE PRESS DISTRIBUTES RECORDINGS of the internationally acclaimed choir *Gloriæ Dei Cantores*, the *Gloriæ Dei Cantores Schola*, and the other instrumental artists of the *Arts Empowering Life Foundation*.

PARACLETE PRESS IS THE EXCLUSIVE NORTH AMERICAN DISTRIBUTOR for the Gregorian chant recordings from St. Peter's Abbey in Solesmes, France. Paraclete also carries all of the Solesmes chant publications for Mass and the Divine Office, as well as their academic research publications.

In addition, PARACLETE PRESS SHEET MUSIC publishes the work of today's finest composers of sacred choral music, annually reviewing over 1,000 works and releasing between 40 and 60 works for both choir and organ.

VIDEO | Our video/DVDs offer spiritual help, healing, and biblical guidance for a broad range of life issues including grief and loss, marriage, forgiveness, facing death, understanding suicide, bullying, addictions, Alzheimer's, and Christian formation.

Learn more about us at our website:
www.paracletepress.com
or phone us toll-free at 1.800.451.5006

SCAN
TO READ
MORE

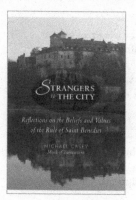
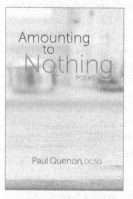